ALSO BY HEATHER McDONALD

You'll Never Blue Ball in This Town Again

MY INAPPROPRIATE LIFE

SOME MATERIAL NOT SUITABLE FOR
SMALL CHILDREN, NUNS, OR MATURE ADULTS

Heather McDonald

A TOUCHSTONE BOOK
Published by Simon & Schuster
New York London Toronto Sydney New Delhi

Touchstone
A Division of Simon & Schuster, Inc.
1230 Avenue of the Americas
New York, NY 10020

First Touchstone hardcover edition February 2013

TOUCHSTONE and colophon are registered trademarks of Simon & Schuster,
Inc.

For information about special discounts for bulk purchases, please contact
Simon & Schuster Special Sales at 1-866-506-1949 or
business@simonandschuster.com.

The Simon & Schuster Speakers Bureau can bring authors to your live event.
For more information or to book an event contact the Simon & Schuster Speakers
Bureau at 1-866-248-3049 or visit our website at www.simonspeakers.com.

Designed by Claudia Martinez

Manufactured in the United States of America

1   3   5   7   9   10   8   6   4   2

Library of Congress Cataloging-in-Publication Data

McDonald, Heather.
My inappropriate life : some material not suitable for small children, nuns, or
mature adults / Heather McDonald.—First Touchstone hardcover edition.
        p. cm
1. McDonald, Heather.   2. Women comedians—United States—Biography.
3. Television personalities—United States—Biography.   I. Title.
PN2287.M5455A3 2013
792.702'8092—dc23
[B]
2012040782

ISBN 978-1-4516-7222-0
ISBN 978-1-4516-7224-4 (ebook)

This book is dedicated to my husband, Peter, and my three children, Mackenzie, Drake, and Brandon. Thank you for understanding that by Mommy revealing a lot about herself and our family in this book we can afford amusement parks, electronics, and 3-D movie tickets.

AUTHOR'S NOTE

This is the memoir of a comedian. There is no one parent, amusement park, birthday party place, etc., quite like the ones that I've described. Names have been changed; characters, locales, and events have been combined, compressed, and reordered. I have exaggerated. I have made some stuff up. That is what I do.

CONTENTS

CONTENTS

FOREWORD

I was going to ask Chelsea to write a foreword, but she is all the way down the hall, so instead I asked my fellow *Chelsea Lately* writers, since they sit right next to me.

There is no one I know who leads a more inappropriate life than my friend Heather. I've personally witnessed her drinking Jamba Juice out of a production assistant's mouth while dressed as Amy Winehouse; she's shot Ping-Pong balls from her nether regions dressed like a Real Housewife; and I've done more sexual positions with her in the name of comedy than I have with half the girlfriends I've had. And all the while, Heather does these things while balancing being the perfect wife, mother, and friend. I hope this book allows you to get to know and fall in love with her the same way I have over the last five years, and I hope I'm still around when Heather has to explain to her youngest son why she was on television French-kissing Fortune Feimster while giving birth to Chuy.

—**Chris Franjola**

Most moms that you work with come to your desk uninvited and start showing you photos or telling you boring stories about their kids, like "Timmy lost a tooth today." Not Heather McDonald. I've never seen a picture of her kids in a school play; instead she shows me photos of her new pool or of the stuffed-animal monkey that she keeps in the car seat in the back of her SUV so that she can ride in the carpool lane to avoid traffic. Or she'll come by to borrow my nail file and then tell me she believes in assisted suicide and is looking to gain residency in states that allow the procedure, or she'll make up a story about my future wherein I move to New York City and decide to be a lesbian for a year. Right now I'm a little nervous that this isn't a very good blurb because I know Heather dreams of reading sentimental things her friends write about her so that she can be moved to tears.

—**Jen Kirkman**

Heather makes no apologies for who she is, and she shouldn't. She's a great mother, wife, coworker, and friend. No matter what's going on, you always know that she loves the people she loves, that if you need her she's going to be there, *and* that she's going to be dressed super-cute. I know it's no secret that she's the center of a lot of jokes at work. But what people may not realize is that she's always in on the joke, and she runs with it. You know if you poke Heather, she's going to respond with something unexpected and hilarious, or a dead-on impression of someone else in the room. She can make a story about going to a coffee shop in Woodland Hills funny, even if all that happened in the story was she went to a coffee shop in Woodland Hills.

To put it simply: I don't know any other person who can tell me they are "over trees," mean it, make me laugh about it, and at the same time make me wonder if perhaps I am too.

—Sarah Colonna

If Heather McDonald was my mom, I would know the difference between a dry white wine and a buttery Chardonnay. If Heather was my mom, I would have a pool and lots of cute summer pool parties. If Heather was my mom, I could always count on her to crack my back because she loves the sound it makes. If Heather was my mom, I would know the names of all the housewives of Orange County, New York, and New Jersey, but probably not Atlanta because she didn't really care for that season. If Heather was my mom, I would have gotten to meet all of the Kardashians by now. And if Heather was my mom, I know that I'd be loved and entertained by her every single day. Heather, you're a hysterical, genuine, and completely original human being. I can't wait to read about all of the ridiculous things that you put your family through.

—Jiffy Wild

Heather McDonald is the most nonphony person in the world. She's unapologetically Heather McDonald and I love her for that. If she's upset because someone else is getting more airtime than she is, she'll literally say, "Why is she getting more airtime than I am?" She cries at work constantly—who doesn't love someone who cries at work! If the world was made up of only Heather McDonalds, there'd be peace on earth (or at least in the West Valley), every backyard would have a nice water feature, and everyone would have a really cute, flat ass.

—Steven Marmalstein

When I first started working at *Chelsea Lately,* Heather McDonald was the last person on earth I thought I'd be friends with. It's not that I didn't like her; she didn't like me! I know, I'm just as shocked as you are. To be fair, they had already gone through two new writers and she was hesitant about investing in a third. Once she realized I wasn't going anywhere, she started to come around. The fact that our boss had just forced us to share an office may have also had something to do with it. I knew I had a lot to live up to, considering her most favorite officemate had been a hilariously witty gay man. Lucky for Heather, I was a laid-back Southern lesbian whose idea of dressing up was throwing a sweater vest over my stained T-shirt and heading for a night out on the town at the Cheesecake Factory. To say we were different would be an understatement. Before long, though, we were gossiping about people in the office, comparing notes about the previous night's *Bachelorette,* and she was asking me, yes me, for advice on which dress she should wear on the roundtable! I was becoming what Heather had been dreaming of . . . a gay man! Now I consider her to be not only a fantastic coworker, who keeps me entertained on a daily basis, but, more important, a friend.

—**Fortune Feimster**

I've had the privilege of working with Heather since day one of *Chelsea Lately.* I thought she was an idiot because she didn't know where to park, and she thought I was gay because I drove a red Mini Cooper. She had a point. Needless to say, it was a rocky start. There were many clashes that ended with her in tears and me having to apologize. Now five years later, I have come to love and respect Heather for who she is—the most sincere, loving, and adoring narcissist ever. But as much of a narcissist as she is, I have to admit that no one was more excited for my wedding or the birth of my son than Heather (and I'm including my wife and myself). She is a true friend with an amazing talent for telling hilarious stories about herself. I'm honored to be included in this foreword, but mostly I'm thrilled that I haven't made her cry in over four years.

—**Brad Wollack**

MY INAPPROPRIATE LIFE

1

THE REAL HOUSEWIVES OF WOODLAND HILLS

Listen, I am the first to admit I am a huge *Real Housewives* fan. I am also proud to say that I never discriminate between the cities in which the action takes place. I will watch the gals from Beverly Hills, Orange County, Atlanta, New Jersey, Miami, and obviously, New York. I even extend my devotion to those lower-caliber shows, like *Mob Wives* and *Basketball Wives,* where the term "wife" is used very loosely. Some days, I wish I wasn't such a wife junkie and could turn to *Downton Abbey* like other, more sophisticated folks—but who are we kidding?

I am so obsessed that I will call my husband, Peter, from my car to make sure he has programmed the TiVo to record the *Real Housewives* and also to make sure that we have chilled Chardonnay for viewing. I prefer to drink while I watch to create a more interactive experience; it helps me relate to the drunk housewives just that much more. This way, I can feel like I'm actually at Beverly Hills' Adrienne Maloof's cocktail party to unveil her new line of platform metal-studded heels. It's just like how my kids prefer participating with their Wii to just watching TV.

Over the years, some of the housewives have become my Facebook friends. I've even met them and shared a meal. And, since they don't eat, I always get to take some leftovers home for Peter. But I don't feel bad about using them for free food. I know the only reason these "wife stars" want to be my friend is because they want to get closer to Chelsea Handler. This happens to me a lot. I tend to think of Chelsea as Jesus and myself as one of her disciples. They're excited to meet Saint James, but who they really want to share that wine and break that bread with is the savior herself. Most of the time,

From our *Real Housewives of New Jersey* reunion parody. I'm playing Danielle Staub.

when they hang out with me, they're really just hoping to be booked as a guest on *Chelsea Lately*. They even get upset when they can't get a booking and will call me to complain. I don't know how much longer I can handle the drunk tears.

Deep down, though, I know where they're coming from. I mean, if you think about it, they've worked so gosh-darned hard to get where they are. Let's take a quick look: first, they had to marry well, then get divorced and marry well *again*. Next, they had to go *all* the way over to the Bravo website and fill out an application. Just think of the concentration required: remembering their Social Security number while also trying to recall their actual birthday. It must all be so taxing.

To be honest, I think *Real Housewives* fame might be just as dangerous as teen-idol fame, if not more so. Six months prior to being booked on the *Real Housewives,* these women's biggest claim to fame was being the hottest mom in the carpool lane at their kid's school, and now they're starring in a prime-time television show and are on the cover of *Life & Style* magazine. And the fact that it happens at the ripe Botoxed age of forty-five makes it that much more difficult for them to handle everything that has become available to them—thus, this delusion of grandeur. OK, I confess, I'm jealous of these women with their one-hit-wonder dance tunes, private wine labels, and wig lines. *They* didn't log in thousands of hours doing stand-up comedy. *They* didn't have to go on hundreds of auditions. *They* never had to be fingered by a William Morris agent through a bodysuit during the '90s.

So you can understand that when I experienced my own unsolicited evening of real housewife–hood it took me by surprise. It was my husband's birthday, which happened to fall on the airing of an *After Lately* episode. This episode was special because my husband and my two sons, Drake and Brandon, had a scene with Chelsea. Since my kids had never been on TV before and were very excited about possibly being recognized at Target, we decided to invite some families over for wine, dinner, and a lively viewing of *After Lately*. My little shindig could hardly compare to the extravagance of a *Real Housewives*–type party, where even brunch requires the hostess to have a stylist help her choose her wardrobe. But I think I did OK when I carefully selected my Hudson jeans with the buttons on the buttocks to make my flat ass cheeks appear less concave, paired with whatever T-shirt was on the top of the folded pile of clean laundry, and gold flats. And why do they all have personal assistants? Again, I'm jealous; I would die for an assistant. That way, my family and close friends would finally receive the thank-you notes they so rightfully deserve.

Peter sent out an Evite and invited four families. This included my very best friend, Liz, whom I met in first grade and her husband, Mark. Also on the list were Anna and Steve, whom we socialize with all the time because their son is Drake's best friend; Ted and Dina, whom we had only hung out with a couple of times so we didn't know well; and Angelina Rose and Bill.

It was a Sunday night, and I had just returned earlier that day from Denver, where I had done six stand-up comedy shows over the weekend, so I was a little tired. Still, I'm always up for a party, and Peter seemed really excited about it too. We ordered some Greek food and I pulled what I like to call a "Kris Jenner" (Momager™ of the Kardashian clan, aka ruler of L.A.) where I transported the take-out dishes from their original foil containers to my personal serving platters. The adults and their kids starting coming around five p.m., but the wine had started flowing for me around four thirty. The kids ran around our backyard and jumped on the trampoline, and the women gathered at my kitchen table and talked about school while the men hung around Peter's new barbecue grill smoker and did guy things.

Let's pause for a moment to discuss Angelina Rose. I know when you hear that name you think stripper, but she isn't. However, for some reason unknown to all of us she never dropped the middle name of Rose. Can you imagine if I was Heather Ann and everyone in my life—all my coworkers, family, and new associates—had to call me Heather Ann and if they just said Heather, I'd politely smile and correct them by saying "It's Heather Ann." How obnoxious would that be? I mean, I have to be honest, sometimes I can't even remember my own kids' middle names. Anyways, I met Angelina Rose a few years earlier when her daughter, Sophia, and my son Drake were at St. Ignatius's preschool together and Angelina Rose coordinated a "Moms' Night Out" at Paoli's Italian Restaurant. Normally, I don't go to Moms' Night Out–type events because they are during the week. After working all day, I just want to spend a couple hours with my kids, but I said yes because it landed on a Tuesday and Tuesdays at Paoli's is karaoke night. I'll take pretty much any opportunity to sing "Something to Talk About" by Bonnie Raitt. I was born with a mike in my hand, and I am one of those freaks who will sing karaoke without drinking (though who'd want to?).

At this time, I had only been working at *Chelsea Lately* full-time for about a year. When I explained what I did for a living, Angelina Rose rolled her eyes and said, "I was in the business for years, but once I became a mother, I just couldn't imagine leaving Sophia with some stranger to raise her while I went off to star in another movie." Now, I watch a lot of movies, but I had never seen this woman outside of the preschool parking lot. "Oh, what have you been in?" I asked, trying to sound interested. "What haven't I been in?" She laughed as she tossed her blond hair about. After fifteen minutes I concluded her last role was a guest spot on the original *Hawaii Five-O*, not the *Hawaii Five-0* with the super-short hot guy who used to be on *Entourage*.

Angelina Rose was very attractive but about eight or nine years older than me, and it was starting to piss me off that she was acting like she turned down the Julianna Margulies role on *The Good Wife* because she didn't want to put Sophia in day care. Her career wasn't going anywhere and hadn't for a while, but I didn't judge (except, yes I did).

I admit, I have a lot of guilt about being gone so much, so I was taking it personally. A lot of moms choose to stay at home because they can afford to, or they always hated their job in insurance (or whatever) and giving birth was their lottery ticket out of cubicle hell. I doubt any stay-at-home mom would choose to stay home if Kelly Ripa's one-hour-a-day job was suddenly offered to them. None of them, even Angelina Rose, would say, "Sorry, I just can't leave my daughter to cohost a national morning talk show. Breakfast is just such a special time for us, and I am the only person who can pour her a bowl of Cinnamon Toast Crunch the way she likes it." Just like no one has ever said, "Heather should be able to bring her kids to work with her every day and have them sit beside her at her desk as she writes jokes about a man in Florida who got caught having sex with a red picnic table." Was I feeling particularly guilty that day about being a working mom? Yes, I believe I was! I had also basically chosen karaoke over reading to my children, so that didn't help how I was interpreting her comments. Sorry, but I'll take singing "I Touch Myself" to an audience at a restaurant over reading *Everybody Farts* to Brandon and Drake for the hundredth time.

Despite Angelina Rose, I still had a great time. Not only because I practically got a standing ovation when I held the word "touch" for fifty-seven seconds, but also because another woman in our group was going through a tumultuous divorce; it made for a very juicy conversation over eggplant Parmesan. I couldn't wait to get home to tell Peter and was taking very meticulous mental notes.

There is nothing that annoys me more than when Peter comes home from playing golf for seven hours with three other men and has no stories to tell me, no scoop, nada. This is how a typical conversation will go.

ME: How was golf?
PETER: Golf? Fine.
ME: Well, did you play fine enough to win any money?
PETER: Yes, eleven dollars.

ME: Great. We'll put that towards our $550 monthly country-club fees. Fiscally, joining the club is really working out. Well, you played with Ted, right?

PETER: Yep. Ted.

ME: Ooooh, what is happening with them? Are they still separated?

PETER: I don't know. We don't talk about that stuff.

ME: What do you mean you don't talk about it? Ted's been your friend for six years. He put a tracking device on the roof of his wife's Range Rover and discovered it was parked at her personal trainer's house for four-hour blocks in the middle of the afternoon every day for two weeks, and she had gained weight. Well, what is up with the personal trainer she had met while in rehab for her addiction to Oxycontin?

PETER: I don't know. I didn't ask.

ME: I didn't either, but somehow I got *your friend* Ted to tell me the whole scandalous made-for-TV Lifetime movie between the piñata and the blowing of five candles at some kid's birthday party. So, let me get this straight. You get to be gone all day and bring absolutely nothing home to entertain me with. How is your golf in any way benefiting me?

Seriously, it's so frustrating. It's not like Peter doesn't love to gossip. I tell him everything that is happening at work and with my single girlfriends, as well as my married girlfriends, and he eats it up like a Gamma Phi Beta sorority sister. I'm sorry, but I think Peter not prying is just downright selfish. The only thing he brings home is his sunburned cheeks that are exasperated by his rosacea, and I'm forced to put Laura Mercier's tinted moisturizer on his face before we leave as a couple to a cocktail party.

I kept running into Angelina Rose at pool and dinner parties, and each time she would tell me what a genius her daughter, Sophia, was and since she felt St. Ignatius was not going to be challenging enough for her they were looking into alternative schools. The kid was fine, but it wasn't like she was playing Beethoven or reading *The Wall Street Journal*. She was just like all the other kids jumping around and whining to get their mom's attention.

One time, at a Halloween party, Angelina Rose was talking about her favorite subject, Sophia, and how she is so smart it's downright scary. My friend Anna was there, talking about her son, Mikey, who is the same age as Sophia, and Angelina Rose interrupted and said mockingly, "I'm sorry, Anna, but I saw Mikey's first-grade homework, and Sophia was doing that same stuff in kindergarten at Whispering Meadows. St. Ignatius is so behind."

The school that Angelina Rose eventually put her daughter into was called Whispering Meadows, and it was three times the price of St. Ignatius and was made up of mostly entertainment-industry families who think their kids poop Pulitzers.

Anyway, the night of my husband's birthday, our evening started while the kids were jumping on the trampoline and Liz, Anna, Dina, Angelina Rose, and I were drinking our wine and wrestling with our lamb shish kebabs. Suddenly Angelina Rose started in again about the new school she had decided to send her so-called genius daughter, and how amazing their abstract-art department is. I mean, isn't all the art that kids do considered abstract? I don't understand abstract art, and half the time I don't know what my boys are attempting to draw. Just then Sophia ran in, whispered something to her mother, and ran back out. Angelina Rose turned to me and said, "Sophia just said that she and Brandon were on the trampoline together and he called her 'lame.'"

I asked, "Are you sure it was Brandon, and not Drake?"

"Yes, she said it was Brandon."

"That's great," I said, straight-faced. "Because last week, when a boy at the park cut in line for the swings, Brandon called him a 'fucking asshole.' Lame is nothing." Anna and Liz burst into laughter, but Angelina Rose and Dina were a little shocked. "Sorry, I just did six stand-up shows in two days," I said.

"Oh my goodness, I don't think Sophia's ever even heard those words," Angelina Rose scoffed.

I was dying to say, *Really? I doubt very much that your husband has never called you a fucking asshole.* But I didn't, because I'm a lady.

After Lately began at eight p.m. Some of the kids were in the playroom, and the others were running in and out of the living room to the backyard as we settled in on the sofa to watch the latest episode. This particular episode featured me having a breakdown over a fight I had with Peter in a writer's meeting. Chelsea invites me to spend the weekend with her at her house to get my mind off it. We become so engrossed watching a Lifetime movie in her bed that she ends up peeing because she doesn't want to miss out on anything in the riveting plot line.

Angelina Rose had poured herself a large glass of Pinot Noir and was completely stretched out on the lounge portion of my sectional couch. A couple minutes into the show, everyone was laughing and I didn't even notice that Sophia had come into the living room. She was standing by her mother's wineglass, watching a scene where Chelsea jokingly asks my colleague Sarah Colonna if she'd brought any drugs to her pool party. Angelina Rose, still taking up the entire bed portion of my couch, said, "Sophia just said to me, 'Mom, this is so inappropriate.' Can you believe that? Even Sophia knows what an inappropriate show this is. Maybe she'll be a TV critic someday." The show resumed and I'm shown getting drunk at Chelsea's house with actresses playing my friends. Once again Sophia comes into the room just as on the show I'm leaning over in an attempt to play Twister and they've edited in a big black square to block out my crotch. Angelina Rose, still lying down, was sipping from her goblet and saying over the roars of laughter, "Oh my God, inappropriate, inappropriate. I can't believe Sophia is seeing this."

At this point I wanted to say, *If you're that concerned, then get off your ass, put down the wine, and take your impressionable genius of a daughter outside to play on the trampoline so she can stop being traumatized by E!'s original programming*, but again I didn't say anything.

When Drake and Brandon's scene was about to come up with Peter and Chelsea, Peter called them in to watch. Once again, Angelina Rose, still lying there, said to the other mother in the room, Dina, "She's going to have her kids watch this? Inappropriate." The boys ran in still holding their Wii remotes, saw themselves say the words "Bye, Chelsea" on TV, and ran out. They're total narcissists, and they had no interest in seeing me, their mother, be hilarious at all. The episode concluded, and the men were all saying how funny it was as the women gathered up the dishes and drinks and headed to the kitchen.

As I walked in, I heard Angelina Rose talking to Dina. She said, "Dina, I just can't believe that show." Dina said, "I know, I don't let my kids watch much TV either because it makes me so uncomfortable."

Angelina Rose continued, "I don't know how I'm going to explain this to Sophia; she's just so smart, it's going to be difficult."

And that's when my *Real Housewives* moment happened. Angelina Rose had caught me on the wrong day. I was coming off of only four hours of sleep, I had consumed three generous glasses of Chardonnay, and it was the day my period was due. I turned with tears in my eyes and said rather loudly, "Well, I'm sorry that the show that puts food in my children's hungry mouths was so inappropriate and it has somehow ruined your parenting plan, but you got the Evite and it clearly stated we'd be watching *After Lately* and not *The Sound of Music.* It wasn't my intention for any of the kids to see it. I thought they'd be preoccupied with violent video games instead."

As I'm saying all this, crying and shaking, I see Peter come around the corner with a look of total shock on his face as if to say, "Shit, what now?" Then my best friend, Liz, comes around the corner. If this were *The Real House-wives of New Jersey,* Liz would be as protective as the matri-arch Caroline Manzo and as angry as Teresa Giudice, ready to flip a table at a moment's notice. "Whoa, whoa, what's going on here, ladies?" Liz asked as she tossed her straight, long blond hair to one side. Meanwhile, Anna didn't know what to do and clearly didn't want to get involved. At this moment I imagined all of us at the Bravo version of *The Real Housewives of Woodland Hills* reunion show, with host Andy Cohen seated in the middle holding his blue cards. It would be at the Woodland Hills Marriott because that is Woodland Hills' most historic hotel, built back in 1986. Sitting on the couch next to me would be Liz, of course, and on the other couch would be Angelina Rose and Dina. Anna would be sitting not as close to the other two, as if to say "I'm Switzerland." Anna would never interrupt and only speak when asked a direct question from Andy Cohen, sent in by a viewer from Beaver Creek, Nebraska. Later it would be announced that Anna chose to leave the show because she wanted to spend more time with her family and her booming candle-making business, but the truth would come out that she was asked not to return because she was so boring and in the history of the Housewives franchise, she was the first woman who honestly didn't like the drama.

I would wear a one-sleeved cranberry-red minidress with gold and diamond hoops and a cuff bracelet—not a ton of bangles, because those clanging bracelets are a nightmare for the sound guy when you're wearing a microphone and they start clanging as you wave your hands to make your point about an untruth someone wrote about you on their blog. I'd pair my dress with my patent-leather nude Jimmy Choo peep-toe heels, highlighting my overly spray-tanned, moisturized legs.

Everyone was frozen. Liz continued, "Angelina Rose, what did you say to Heather? What happened, Heather?" The hostess in me came back out and said, "No, it's nothing, it's just I didn't mean for the kids to see *After Lately* and some (really only one, but I didn't want to point it out) of them did and I'm sorry. I'm really sorry." Then Angelina Rose said, "It's fine, Heather. Everyone makes mistakes." She went to hug me, but my hands were wiping my tears away so she just stood there and held me awkwardly. I tried to end the hug by pulling away, but she kept on hugging me in a tight hold. Thank God her normal husband had the good sense to gather their coats and was standing there ready to leave. Dina apologized to me, saying that her kids didn't see any of it and that she felt bad that she said anything about it.

Once all the families had left, Peter asked, "God, what happened? Why did you get so upset and start crying?" Now, this question really pissed me off because after eleven years of marriage he should know to shut up and be on my side. I said, "OK, Peter, when you come back to earth as a woman and you've had four hours of sleep and three glasses of wine on the day before your period, and another woman criticizes your profession and your parenting over and over again in your home and you choose not to cry, then you can criticize my behavior tonight!"

Liz called me the next morning as I was driving to work and said, "You know what that whole thing was about, don't you? Angelina Rose was jealous. She is an out-of-work actress. She would die to be starring on a TV show, and here you are on not only one show, but two. She is not happy with the decisions she's made in her life and the only way she can deal with it is trying to make a happy, confident person like you question your decisions."

I started to feel a little sorry for Angelina Rose and made a conscious effort to let the whole thing go. That is, until a few hours later when I checked my Facebook page, where, by the way, I have the maximum of 5,000 friends. That includes all my real friends and fans, all of whom I accepted until it got to the maximum (I now have a fan page, so feel free to Like me). Lo and behold, right there on my Facebook wall was a message from Angelina Rose. She wrote: "Heather, thanks for the great dinner and wine last night. Being a mother can be so trying sometimes and it's obvious from last night that you are having a very difficult time with it. I will continue to pray for you."

OK, that was it! I no longer felt sorry for her. The first thing I did was remove the post. The second thing I did was to call Peter and tell him about it. I said, "The good news is, I'm not under some contract with Bravo. Therefore, *The Real Housewives of Woodland Hills* does not exist so producers cannot legally force me to hang out with this woman so we can be filmed together. We are not going to socialize with Angelina Rose and her husband, and she will never step foot in my home or on my trampoline ever again! Got it?" Peter responded with a resounding shrug of his shoulders and mild concern that we would be losing out on a gossip source.

2

GOING BANANAS

I live only eighteen miles from the *Chelsea Lately* offices, but in order to get there, I have to take an L.A. freeway called the 405. Everyone hates this drive because the 405 is always so backed up and has been going through construction for the past four thousand years. On a day where we shoot two shows, I have to be at the studio by eight forty-five a.m. One Wednesday, I was just about to get on the freeway when I remembered I was scheduled to be on the roundtable on the show. I had completely forgotten and therefore forgot to pack a cute dress to wear. The show does not provide wardrobes for us, and I was wearing one of my classic velour Juicy Couture sweatsuits in rust. There was no way I could wear that on TV, and besides, rust is not a particularly flattering color on anyone. I quickly did an illegal U-turn and headed back. I ran into the house, picked the first dress I saw, and grabbed a pair of black heels. As

I was running back past Brandon's room, I saw Brandon—or what I thought was Brandon. In that quick second I thought I was losing my mind. I knew Peter had dropped off the kids that morning . . . did he forget Brandon? I took a second look and realized it was the toddler-size monkey that Kris Jenner gave all the kids at her Christmas Eve party. The kids had put a T-shirt and Brandon's Red Sox hat from his T-ball team on the monkey, and at a glance he looked like a real child. I suddenly realized that if I strapped this monkey in Brandon's car seat I could take the carpool lane on the 405. I made sure that his seat belt was secure, stuffed his monkey ears into the cap, and added a scarf because it looked cute, and layering is in.

My fourth child.

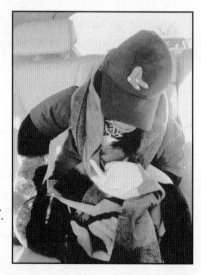

Now layered with a scarf.

As I first merged into the carpool lane, my heart was beating and I kept looking in my rearview mirror at my "child" in the backseat and to make sure no cops were tailing me. It was 8:31 a.m. and by 8:40 I was getting off at my exit. It was amazing how I flew down the freeway. I was never going back to using regular lanes.

The next morning we were not taping a show, so I had the time to drive the kids to school. When the three of them piled in, Brandon got very upset when he saw his monkey in the car. I didn't want to tell the kids the truth for fear that they would say something to their teachers about how their mother broke the law, so I said, "I like him in my car. It makes me feel like I have a fourth child [Mackenzie, my stepdaughter now also lived with us]. I don't get so lonely when I'm driving to work." Something in my explanation really set off Brandon and he said, "I don't want him wearing my Red Sox hat. That's mine!" Brandon ripped it off of his head. "Fine," I said. When the kids got out at the school drop-off, I noticed the baseball hat on the floor of the backseat and without even thinking about it I put it back on the monkey. When I got on the 405 with my fourth child, even though I wasn't pressed for time, I found myself merging in the carpool lane with less trepidation.

When the kids got in my car the next morning, Brandon yelled, "Why is that monkey wearing my T-ball hat again? He's not even on the team!" This made Mackenzie and Drake burst into laughter, which only got Brandon more upset. "I hate that monkey," he cried. Mackenzie continued to tease him: "Brandon, don't say that about your little brother." Brandon folded his arms and huffed. Could it be that Brandon, the baby of the family, was actually worried that the stuffed monkey would take his place?

I'm the youngest of five and my dad adored me, by always giving me tons of attention. When he scolded me for the very first time, I remember my brother Jim started a slow clap, like the kind you see at the end of every 1980s John Hughes film. Jim said to my three other siblings, "Finally the favorite gets in trouble too. Justice is served." I started to cry and my dad picked me up as I stuck my tongue out at the others.

I remember when I was six and invited Liz (my best friend from basically birth) to join our family at a basketball game. Something changed between my dad and me. When she arrived, she was wearing satin hot-pink dolphin shorts and a matching satin jacket. I was so jealous of her cool outfit. Then, halfway through the game, she asked my dad if she could sit on his lap. When we were walking to our car, she took his hand. My dad thought it was sweet, but I could have killed my best friend in a crime of passion. The way I saw it, my dad was cheating on me with another six-year-old little girl and doing it right in front of my face. I walked ahead of them and yelled, "Why don't you just adopt her, Dad, if you like her so much better than me?" My dad thought it was hysterical. To this day, my dad brings it up when he sees Liz. The two of them still share a special bond. Needless to say, I understood where Brandon was coming from. But this monkey was not another boy; it was a stuffed animal that was saving me twelve to eighteen minutes a day on my commute. I didn't care how upset Brandon got. That monkey was just too precious for me to give up.

The next week, Monkey and I flew down the 405. Well, we didn't fly. Instead of going an average of eight miles an hour we were going seventeen, but it did allow for me to stop at Starbucks and get coffee before my writers' meeting began. On those drives in I started to fantasize about having another child. I always felt like Brandon was a baby until recently, when I was having a dinner party and I kept referring to him as the baby. One of the guests asked, "So where is your baby? Is it sleeping?" I answered, "No. It's that huge thing over there writing on an iPad." I knew Peter didn't want more kids, but if I was to have a child now, things would be so different than with Drake and Brandon. For one thing, we have more money, so we could afford a full-time nanny, who could even bring the baby by the office for quick visits. And being slightly known in basic cable can be huge in the baby world. My publicist worked with *Playboy*'s Kendra Wilkinson when she had her baby, so he has all the connections for free maternity clothes and free baby clothes. I can see the spread now of the nursery in *In Touch*. I could take photos of myself with no makeup on and my chin squished into my neck to look really fat and secure a Nutrisystem endorsement deal. Me on the cover of *OK* in a pink bikini, spray-tanned to the hilt, wearing nude strappy heels and holding the baby so its chunky legs would fall perfectly and cover my love handles squirting over the top of my bikini bottom. I know exactly how to pose and tilt my hip to make me look the thinnest. I'd feed this baby only organic food and have the nanny make the baby food in one of those special baby blenders. I would exploit it not just to benefit me and my career but our whole family. If only I could convince

Peter that a new baby would help his golf game or get him a set of free clubs, he'd be just as gung-ho as me.

This is what I wear to Target when
I just need a little pick-me-up.

By the second week, the kids were getting used to sharing the backseat with the monkey, and even Brandon seemed resigned. See, I thought, Brandon will be able to accept not being the baby anymore. I think a new baby is really the way to go. That night I had to take Mackenzie to Target to get something for school. When we got out of the car in the parking lot and locked it with my remote, she said to me, "But Mom, you're leaving your baby in the car." I just laughed and said, "He's OK. He's sleeping and we'll only be a minute." When I got up to the front of the store where the solicitors with their petitions are, I heard a woman's voice behind me say, "Excuse me, miss. I'm sorry, I don't normally do this." At that point I thought, Yes, it's me, I'm the girl from *Chelsea Lately* and *After Lately*. Thanks for watching E! This happens a lot to me at my local Target. People approach me all the time, and not just when I'm wearing a red shirt and tan pants, which can be annoying when all they really want from you is to know what aisle the Swiffers are in. As I turned to her with a smile, anticipating a compliment and a request for a photo of us taken on her camera phone, she said, "You cannot leave your child sleeping in your car. It's over ninety degrees out. You're lucky I didn't call 911." Oh my God, she'd heard Mackenzie and me joking. "No, that's a stuffed monkey. It's not a real boy," I said. She continued, "Look, I won't call the police if you get him out right now!" Everyone was staring at us, including the people collecting signatures for a petition to get the local pound to serve only organic dog food. She went on: "I don't believe you. I'm going to follow you to your car."

Since when do people get so nosy? My mom left us alone in the car all the time. I was just thankful that she remembered to pick us up from Rollerrama in the first place. Maybe this woman saw too many episodes of ABC's *Primetime: What Would You Do?* with John Quiñones, where hidden cameras capture real people responding to outrageous behavior by actors who are hired by ABC. Oftentimes the actors are overly pushy or neglectful parents and the show captures a concerned citizen stepping in and then later revealing to them that it was all a setup and congratulating them on getting involved. Seriously, I knew this woman wasn't going to let up, so I said, "Here, please come and see for yourself." When I opened the car and pointed to the monkey, Mackenzie chimed in, "My mom uses him so she can ride in the carpool lane on the 405 to work. She's on *Chelsea Lately*." I didn't know what was more horrifying, that the woman who was questioning me was an African American, or that Mackenzie was selling me down the river.

"Mackenzie, that's not true," I said with a smile. "Then why did you tell us that?" Mackenzie asked. My heart was beating so fast. I imagined myself in an interrogation room at the police department and what it would look like when they put it on *48 Hours Mystery*. How I would look being shot from above with the surveillance camera? How many hours could I go on lying until I'd finally break and admit to the crime? More important, if I were to be arrested, would I be famous enough for my mugshot to appear on *TMZ*? Maybe not the TV show but possibly TMZ.com. I believe at least it would be posted up there for a good part of an afternoon. I've been practicing my mugshot face since Lindsay Lohan was arrested for her second DUI back in 2007. It's a soft, closed-mouth smile, and I tilt my head slightly to the left with big innocent eyes so I still look pretty but somewhat regretful for what put me behind bars—even if it was a simple misunderstanding.

The woman who walked me to the car said, "I'm sorry. I feel like such an idiot," and walked off. I turned to Mackenzie. "I told you never to tell anyone about the carpool lane," I said firmly. "I'm sorry; I didn't want her to think you were a bad mom," she said as she started to cry. I felt terrible. Here my beautiful stepdaughter was just trying to protect me. That night I removed the monkey from my backseat for good.

About a month later, we read in the *Los Angeles Times* that an old friend of ours, whom we hadn't seen in years other than his Christmas card, pled guilty to tax fraud and was facing hard time. Peter turned to me and said seriously, "That's why I don't want you ever driving with that monkey in the carpool lane."

"I told you he's out of my car, back living in Brandon's room. But do you know how you can never have to worry about me illegally going into the carpool lane again?" I said coyly.

"How?" he asked.

"Give me a new baby," I said.

He thought for a second and then said very dryly, "I'd rather you go to prison."

3

THE NINE STEPS OF BEING KICKED IN THE ASS BY SUZE ORMAN

At *Chelsea Lately,* we were able to get financial guru Suze Orman to come in and film her giving a few of the writers financial advice. I was lucky enough to be one of them, or so I thought. She seemed nice enough and she had extremely white teeth, which highlighted her Suze hair. We started talking, and I immediately liked her. I stared at the infamous one pair of earrings Suze owns; she only bought one pair of earrings in her whole life, and that's why she is so wealthy. (Can you imagine opening up a lemonade stand with her as a kid? She would be so serious, keeping books, not giving samples, and talking all the time about how she wanted to expand.) Appropriately, her earrings were gold balls.

Suze said, "What can I help you with?"

My question for Suze was "Can my husband and I afford a fourth child?"

She said, "Do you own your own home?" speaking in Suze voice.

I proudly said, "Yes!"

"How much do you owe on it?"

I said, "Well, our loan is for more than the house is worth, but isn't that everyone's situation today, except for you and Oprah?"

Suze said, "What are the terms of your rate?"

I said, "I know it's thirty-year fixed. I don't know the rate, but my husband told me it was a really good one."

Suze went apeshit.

She asked, "What does your husband do?"

I replied, "He's a mortgage broker and a Realtor."

She became incensed. "So your husband the mortgage broker and the Realtor put you in a home that is now worth less than you paid. Do you have any stocks?"

"Yes," I said proudly.

Suze asked me, "Who are they with?"

I said, "I don't know. The statements come with an envelope that reads 'LPL' on it."

She grew red. "What the hell is LPL?"

I grew red, and said, "Well, I don't know, but I could call my husband at home and ask."

Suze asked, "He works from home?"

I said, "Well, he has been trying to sell his one listing for the past eighteen months, which says a lot about the owners still really liking his service."

Suze shook her head and then asked, "Do you have life insurance?"

I said, "Yes. He has a million dollars on me, but I only have $500,000 on him. Do you think I should be suspicious?"

Suze barked back, "No. He doesn't make any money. You don't need it."

Suze then wanted to know about some of my other expenses.

I said, "Our children go to private school, and Peter has a golf membership for $550 a month." I was a little scared about admitting the second one.

Suze immediately tore into the golf membership. "Don't you think you should take that $550 a month and pay off your home loan?"

I said, "He really enjoys it. Even when he goes to a charity auction, he always bids and wins to play rounds of golf at other country clubs in our area. So not only is he familiar with all the other golf courses, he's also quite a philanthropist!"

Suze was dumbfounded and couldn't speak for a minute.

Suze then said, "Well, you're generous with him. Is he generous with you?"

I said, "He never makes any comments on what I spend on clothes. But I've asked him when he grocery shops to please buy fresh-squeezed orange juice, which he refuses to do."

She said, "I agree. Looking at your finances, you can't afford it, nor do you deserve it." Then she asked me, "How is he with the children?"

I said, "Well, I ask him to buy organic milk for the kids because there are so many hormones in the regular kind, and if you buy that your daughter will get her period at four. Our daughter is twelve and she still hasn't gotten her period. I think it's because of the organic milk."

Suze said (again in Suze voice but this time much louder and firmer), "Your daughter is twelve and she still hasn't gotten her period? Well, I'll tell you why she hasn't. She hasn't gotten her period because she is so stressed out that her mother knows nothing about her family's finances."

She continued, "Let me tell you about a woman I met. She and her husband were at a flower store. It was their one-year wedding anniversary. She turned to look at a tulip, and when she turned back around he had *dropped dead* just like that. She had no clue where their money was, the terms of their insurance policy, or their debts, let alone what their mortgage rate was. I cannot tell you how many countless crying widows I have counseled who all have the same story: My husband took care of it. Well, guess what? He can't take care of it when he's six feet under. What if tomorrow Peter goes out to the golf course and on the ninth hole he *drops dead* just like that? I'll tell you, you'll have more problems than having fresh-squeezed orange juice to worry about. I can't tell you how many women have rolled over in the middle of the night to feel their husband's icy-cold deceased body lying next to them and they don't even know where the key to the safety-deposit box is. Heather, what if Peter choked on a chicken bone in the middle of dinner, clutching his throat as he takes his final breaths and *drops dead*? Do you have any idea how much your water bill is each month?"

I said, "No. Don't they bundle it with the electric?"

Suze shook her head and said, "How are you going to live

on Peter's $500,000 life insurance with not just three, but four kids?"

I said, "Suze, actually you've helped me decide to not go ahead with that fourth child, since Peter is going to *drop dead* at any moment."

That night I went home with a clipboard with all of Suze's questions. I gave it to Peter to fill out. He said he would look into it the next day. And I said, "Over your dead body. You'll do it tonight!"

4

B.C.

When you're raising a boy, you inevitably begin to notice that every girl around your son's age seems smarter, more verbal, and just generally is more on top of shit. That's because they are. Unfortunately, I didn't come to this particular realization until my son Brandon's behavior began confounding the preschool teachers. According to them, he often climbed on the outside of the jungle gym, jumped off into the woodchip pile, and got hurt. But then he would just cry alone for a bit and go back and do it again. The teachers grew concerned that he wasn't feeling pain properly, and so couldn't correctly gauge the danger of his actions. On first hearing this, I couldn't help but wonder how their line of thinking would work in a football game; the minute anyone got sacked, they'd just have to quit. But the week before, Brandon had climbed over our booth at P.F. Chang's, fell into another couple's laps, laughed, and stolen their chocolate-covered fortune cookie. Maybe a little lesson in consequences wouldn't hurt. So I took their report very seriously and decided to have him evaluated.

Unfortunately, I left the report out one night when my parents came over to babysit. When Peter and I returned from dinner, my dad instantly wanted to talk about it. And by talk about it, I mean recruit my four-year-old son to the Marine Corps. "That boy is great! He just doesn't give up. He'd make a perfect Marine." My dad was a combat Marine in World War II, played college football, and likes to say he comes from the greatest generation that ever lived. I patiently explained that we actually weren't very happy about the report because the teachers were concerned that he didn't feel pain properly and had difficulty evaluating danger. My father just smiled and said, "That's the kind of fearlessness that the Marine Corps looks out for when choosing those few good men." My mother, however, went crazy in an entirely different way. "Does this mean they won't let him into St. Ignatius's kindergarten?" I said, "I don't know, Mom. If it's not the right school for him, I'm not going to force him to go there." My mother, being the open-minded woman she is, said, "Well, there is no better school than St. Ignatius. It's the number-one school in the Catholic Los Angeles Archdiocese. There's no way he's going to the public school. What's he going to do? Go to school in a flak jacket? Because that's what they do now. I read it in the *L.A. Times*. Besides, he's not bilingual; he wouldn't understand the teachers. I think I saw that on Fox News!"

We were getting ahead of ourselves. When I first began looking into schools for Brandon, I visited CHARM, a public school where normal kids learn side by side with physically and mentally handicapped children. I figured it was a safe bet since I wasn't yet sure which side my child was on. Desperate that Brandon would have no school to go to, I offered the admissions officers tickets to *Chelsea Lately,* claimed I could get Chelsea to sign books for them, and promised to shower them in Chuy Bravo bobbleheads. Driving out of the parking lot, I looked around at the other students, and thought, Brandon might actually have a chance here. To boost his self-confidence, he could play kickball with the wheelchair-bound children.

This actually wasn't the first time I doubted Brandon's ability to play on a regular baseball team like his older brother, Drake. A few summers back, I had been cutting a Dodgers cake for Drake and his teammates when another mother alerted me to an inert Brandon lying facedown on the concrete. Flinging down the knife, I sprinted to his side and picked him up, but he just stared at me and didn't say anything. As another parent quickly called 911, I grabbed Drake by his uniform, pulled him in front of Brandon, and asked, "What is his name, what is his name?" Brandon looked blankly at Drake and didn't answer. My heart pounding, I cried out, "He doesn't even remember his brother's name!" Another boy stepped up behind me, and I heard Drake say, "Mom, I'm right here." Slowly looking up at the boy I had trapped in my vise-like grip, I realized I had not managed to grab my own son. Even I didn't know this kid's name. I let go and nervously patted out the newly formed wrinkles in No-Name's shirt while Brandon calmly explained to Drake that he had simply been trying to lick some spare bubblegum off the pavement. On second thought, those wheelchair kids might have given Brandon a run for his money on the kickball field.

The second school I visited was a half hour from our home, compared to the three-minute drive to St. Ignatius. This school only had normals, and since they had a bunch of graduate students teaching there, the ratio of students to teachers was extremely low, meaning Brandon would get the attention he was quickly beginning to prove he needed. I liked it a lot, so I decided to bring Peter and Brandon there to see if they liked it too. The whole way there, Peter wouldn't stop complaining about how far away it was. According to him, if there was an earthquake, and we broke off into our own island, it would take precisely ten days for us to reach Brandon. My mother had of course read in the *L.A. Times* that this disaster was imminent, and constantly reminded us to be prepared. I figured I could just hunker down in her wine cellar/garage, which was already stocked with Chardonnay and canned goods. Plus, her pool was purified, so we could make a killing bottling the water and selling it to the neighbors.

At the school we visited a kindergarten class was already in session. In a year Brandon would be learning these same things that were being taught in the classroom. As I was talking to the teacher, Brandon finally put on his A-game and began reading off every single sight word on the blackboard. We got the application and told the administrator that we were going to discuss it, and that we'd get back to her. However, seconds after we pulled out of the parking lot, Peter said, "We're not going there, or to the first school, because there's nothing wrong with him. I'm not driving him all this way, so if St. Ignatius's doesn't take him, he's going to our public school just down the street. I don't care what your mother reads in the *L.A. Times!*"

The next day at work, I was upset about Brandon's situation, so I wisely decided to confide in Chris Franjola, who has no kids and is the biggest playboy on staff. "Apparently Brandon's teachers say he doesn't like to hold a pencil and prefers the iPad," I said. "I just spent $150 on supplies from a website called Handwriting without Tears. Why did I name him Brandon? That's seven letters. If I had named him Max or Bo, surely he would have been able to write his name by now." Chris paused, looked at me, and said, "I don't fucking get it. Why use a pencil when you have a fucking iPad? The kid must be real smart." This cheered me up, so I decided to call the principal, Mrs. Walls, at St. Ignatius to talk about Brandon and find out if there was a patron saint of holding a pencil whom I could start praying to.

I tried to explain to her how much I had enjoyed my own Catholic education and wanted my second son to be able to experience it and have spirituality and prayer on a daily basis, but all she heard was: "Black cock."

I should pause and quickly explain a common practice that goes on with my colleagues at work. Whenever one of us is on a business call, or on with a doctor, someone will scream out an obscenity. "Black cock" happens to be the all-time favorite.

Mrs. Walls apparently did not know the proper response to this exclamation, so I pretended I had a cough and said, "OK, see you next Tuesday," and hung up.

That evening I went to a seminar on "How Boys and Girls Learn Differently." The instructor stated that girls were scoring higher in every single subject in every country and it's because their brains work differently. He described it as a girl's brain having a highway of multiple lanes going in different directions and converging and merging, making them much better at multitasking and therefore making them better students.

On the other hand, a male brain is just a sad, two-lane highway, where they can be easily distracted and end up in a big pileup.

He said that males typically hear better out of one ear, usually the right one. They don't take in information as well when you are talking directly to them, but rather do absorb it if you sit next to their right ear. This started to make sense to me because when you are standing in front of them talking, men are distracted by your boobs, but in the car they retain more information.

When it comes to learning, boys do best when they're seated up close and by a sunny window and you have to constantly feed them water. I started to wonder, Is this a plant or a child we are talking about? The instructor went on to explain that boys are inherently attracted to violence, and you should embrace and not discourage their weapon play. At this point I was wishing I had only given birth to girls.

As the seminar continued, everything about my boys' behavior was making perfect sense. Several friends and family members have commented when they witness my boys wrestling and trying to shoot at each other, "Well, at least they're not gay." This offends me because I would kill to have a gay son to go shoe shopping with. Can't at least one of them be gay? I thought. Who else is going to take me to a fancy brunch every Sunday twenty years from now?

I came home and I sat next to Peter and his right ear, handed him a glass of water, and relayed the information I had learned. I said, "When we speak to the principal at St. Ignatius on Tuesday, I'm really going to fight to get Brandon in and tell her all the reasons he should be there."

"Whatever you do, please don't start crying in the middle of the meeting" was Peter's reply.

My mother called the night before the meeting and said, "You just march in there and you remind them how much money your parents gave to help rebuild the church after the 1994 earthquake."

Peter and I took separate cars to the meeting, as I had to go to work afterward and Peter works from home. I got there first and calmly said to Mrs. Walls, "I think that Brandon should go to St. Ignatius's kindergarten because . . ." And then my nostrils started to quiver, my mouth started to turn down, as I said, "We're a Catholic family and we need to stay together. Peter and I were married here, I went to school here, you can't separate Brandon from his big brother, Drake." And then I spiraled. "Also, anytime you want, if you have a niece in town who's a big fan, I can get you tickets to

Chelsea Lately and have Chelsea sign books for you. Plus they can ride on Chuy's motorized scooter . . ."

She deadpanned, "What's *Chelsea Lately?*"

I said, "Oh, it's the late-night talk show I work on. It's on E!"

She said, "E! What's that? I don't watch cable, just PBS."

There was no stopping the elephant tears now, and of course Peter walked in to see me with mascara running down my face. "Oh no, Heather. Really?" he said.

I blubbered on. "My point is that I'm dedicated to this school. I'm not like other parents here. I'm never going to go to a private, nondenominational school, even if I get my own sitcom on Fox, which, by the way, is channel eleven here, just nine away from PBS."

Brandon on his first day of kindergarten
at St. Ignatius. You can see how happy
I am that he got accepted.

Peter thankfully jumped in and said, "Look, Mrs. Walls, there's nothing wrong with Brandon. He just needs the summer to grow up, and he'll be fine in the fall."

"Yes, I agree with you, Peter," she miraculously replied. "He did fine on the entrance exam. And I have his acceptance letter right here."

Now, I try not to get so upset about the bumps in my kids' elementary education. Brandon holds a pencil now. The other day Drake's third-grade teacher showed me his school-issued iPad and his report on safaris, showing me everything he had researched on the Internet. It read, "How many rings around Saturn, Abraham Lincoln, boobs, capital of California, poo, Martin Luther King Jr., and sexual innuendos." The last one concerned her, but I said, "Wow, Drake can spell 'innuendo'?"

5

MY PERSONAL STYLIST

I adore Vera Wang. She is over sixty, looks amazing, has hair to her waist, and is a size 0. I was positively vibrating when I saw that she was going to be an interview guest on the show. A couple of weeks before she was scheduled to come to the studio, Tom, our executive producer, said, "Hey, give your dress sizes to Deb, because Vera wants to give you and Sarah Colonna some dresses to wear on the round table."

I waited for Deb to follow up and, so un-Vera of me, I simply forgot about it. I never handed over my size info.

A few days later we had a fire drill that brought us to the parking lot. Tom said to me, "Why didn't you ever give Deb your measurements? They're sending a bunch of stuff to Sarah."

It was one of the worst days of my life. I ran up to Deb and said, "I'm so sorry I forgot! I'm a four . . . can you relay that to Vera's people?"

Deb said, "It's a little late now. I mean, next week's the Oscars. I'm sure she's busy."

I said, "OK. Well, see what you can do."

Deb promised she would call Vera's publicist the next day.

A couple of hours later as I was making copies of a script for a sketch outside of Sarah's office, I heard her say on the phone, "Joe, just open the box. . . . Are there four dresses in there? I can't wait to see them when I get home tonight."

Sarah hung up the phone and I asked her, "Did the Vera Wang dresses get sent to your house?"

She replied, "Yeah. Joe says there are also three pairs of shoes. I'm so happy because now I definitely have something to wear to the E! after-party that we're hosting post-Oscars."

I thought I was going to throw up. Why hadn't I given Deb my measurements? Maybe it was karma paying me back for the day I lied and called in and said I couldn't make it to work because my sewer pipe broke and I was drowning in feces.

Later I went into Chelsea's office, and on her computer screen was a photo of her on a red carpet. I said, "Wow, that's a cute dress." It was navy-blue satin, strapless, and fitted. She said, "Oh, it's Vera Wang."

I said, "Oh my God, you're making me sicker." Then I told Chelsea the story. I did bag on Deb for her failure to remind me, even though it was my fault entirely.

Chelsea was like, "Well, it's not great."

———————

It was now a few days before the Oscars, and I had no time to go to Bloomingdale's and look for a dress. So when I realized that I'd missed out on a figure-flattering, age-appropriate dress and Sarah was all set with her outfit, it just made me sick. The next day, the Thursday before the Sunday Oscars, Deb stopped me in the hallway and said she spoke to Vera's people and there was a chance, but only a slight chance, that she might be able to get some dresses to me.

I couldn't thank Deb enough. I was ecstatic. Just like Disney, Vera Wang dreams do come true!

A couple of hours later I was watching a clip that we were considering putting in the show, and Deb came running in. "Heather, Vera Wang is on my phone right now and wants to talk to you."

I jumped up and ran back with her to her office. Deb said, "Here, come sit on my exercise ball and talk into the speakerphone." Deb pressed the button and said, "Vera, I have Heather here for you."

I heard in a slightly affected Upper East Side accent with a little British thrown in, "Hello, Heather."

I said, "Hello, Vera. It's so nice to speak with you."

Vera said, "I hear you need a dress for the Oscars."

I replied, "Well, yes, but I'm not going to the Oscars. I'm just doing a little TV hosting gig on E!"

She said, "Oh," and sounded a little bit disappointed. I mean, I have a good career, but I'm not exactly in the Oscar-presenter league.

"I really just need a cocktail dress," I said. "Knee-length is fine. I loved the navy dress of yours that Chelsea wore the other night."

She asked me if my figure was like Chelsea's.

I said, "Well, we're both a size four, but she's a more athletic build. I have bonier arms and legs."

She said, "Would you say your figure is like Angelina Jolie's?"

I was taken aback. I said, "Well, I'm not that slim, and I don't have tattoos. I like strapless, but not when it's so tight against the skin where you get a vagina-armpit look." I said this with a girly giggle, hoping we would bond, but Vera was silent. And I thought, Hmm. Vera doesn't have much of a sense of humor.

Vera then said, "What's your red-carpet style?"

I replied, "I'm pretty put-together."

Vera said in a bit of a huff, "I'm trying to get a sense of who you are. What kind of animal would you be on the red carpet?"

I had to think about that one. And finally I confided in Vera, "I'm really not into animals. I'm definitely not a cougar, maybe a giraffe?"

She asked, "Are you available in the next hour? Because I can send my assistant over to fit you."

I said, "Oh, of course, I'll be here," as I mouthed to Deb, *This is so amazing!*

Vera then said, "All I ask is that you agree to go on our website in the dresses."

I said, "Vera, my pleasure. I love websites!"

She said, "OK. I'll send my assistant over with two dresses, and whichever one you don't wear to the Oscars you can keep and wear another time and go up on our website for that one too. All I need from you right now is a credit card. The total will be thirteen thousand dollars."

For a moment I thought she was joking, but then I remembered she had no sense of humor.

My Vera dreams came to a bitter crash. How could she think I could afford $13,000? I work for E!

I said, "I'm sorry, I can't afford that."

She was like "Oh," and right then a camera crew came into the office, followed by all the *Chelsea* writers and Tom, our executive producer. Everybody was laughing at me and then they brought in Sarah Colonna and said, "Meet Vera." It was a total prank, from the start. They had little cameras hidden all over Deb's office.

My only retort was "So I still don't have a dress to wear to the Oscar party?"

That night instead of being fitted by Vera's apprentice, the nice saleswoman at Nordstrom rang me up for a silver beaded cocktail dress that was $12,800 cheaper than "Vera's."

6

PLAYMATE MOM OF THE YEAR

I first met Nala back in 2006 outside of Drake's and Brandon's preschool. She was a natural brunette mom close to my age with olive skin and green eyes. I knew her kids, but she was kind of a mystery, she had two full-time nannies who brought her twins to school and to Mass on Sundays. But when I did finally run in to her, we instantly hit it off because she wanted to talk about my favorite subject—me possibly selling her house. I had been working in residential real estate since I was twenty to supplement my occasional auditions for a guest spot on a sitcom. It's a great business for moms because you can make your own hours, and it enables you to be with your kids a lot. Nala and I exchanged phone numbers and when I got her address I immediately looked it up. It was a very large house for the neighborhood and she had said she wanted to get something smaller. Great, I thought. That meant potentially two sales.

That night I called her to set up an appointment to take a closer look at her house and discuss what I thought she should list it for. Within the first minutes of the conversation she really opened up and was quite amazing to talk to. She told me how when she was twenty-one she was actually in *Playboy*. I mentioned how I used to go to the mansion parties but once I got married and asked to bring my husband, they said no, and then stopped sending me invitations. Nala said how she and her husband still go all the time and she could get Peter and I both in as her guests. I guess spreading it all for *Playboy* has its privileges. She had met Ron, an investment banker, five years earlier and they got married after dating for just a few months. Ron was twenty-four years older than Nala. We must have talked for three hours that first night. We discovered that we hung out at all the same hot spots back in the day, and even had partied with several of the same Hollywood fixtures. However, I guessed that I had ended up in my own bed far more often than she had. I kept trying to get back to the selling of her house, but she didn't really want to talk about it. In fact, she said, "Let's have a playdate first with the kids. Come over at one p.m. on Tuesday with Drake. He can play with the twins, and you can see the house, and we can get to know each other better before we get into all the business stuff." Perfect, I thought. Tuesdays were the day I had help, so I decided to leave Brandon with the nanny and have my playdate/business meeting.

When Drake and I arrived on Tuesday, a cute girl in her twenties, who was one of Nala's nannies, came out to greet us. She was very nice and welcomed us in. After about fifteen minutes of no Nala I asked, "Is Nala here?"

"No," replied the nanny, "but she said she's on her way." After an hour of being Nala-less, I started to get annoyed. I didn't go there to hang out with a twenty-year-old nanny. I could have left Drake with Brandon and our nanny, the one I was paying, and actually gotten some work done. Once it got to be three p.m. and Drake was getting a little cranky, I said, "Well, we're going to get going." As I was driving out of her cul-de-sac, Nala was coming in. She rolled down her window to talk and said, "Hey, girl, where ya going?"

"Oh, Drake is tired," I said.

"Sorry I'm late, but I ran into this guy who used to go to my gym and he really needed to talk." If it weren't for a potential commission, I would have never spoken to her again. *A guy who used to go to her gym?* What the fuck kind of excuse was that? It was so rude. But I put a nice smile on my face and told her how beautiful I thought her home was.

A few days later, I called Nala in an attempt to have a meeting with her husband about listing their house. Somehow that conversation turned into a girls' night at the Mexican restaurant down the street from her house. She encouraged me to invite my friends, so I invited Liz and my other best friend Tara. The plan was that I'd pick Nala up at her home and then we'd meet Tara and Liz at the restaurant at 7:30. At 7:15 I rang her bell. I was pretty excited to go out. I had lost almost all the baby weight and was wearing a new black dress. Her husband opened the door. He definitely looked well into his sixties and not particularly attractive, but he was very nice. He said, "Nala's getting ready. Here, I'll show you to her room." We passed what was clearly the master bedroom and he pointed to another room and said, "Nala, your friend Heather is here." I walked in and there she was, going through a pile of clothes unable to decide what to wear. This bedroom looked just like what you used to see on E!'s *The Girls Next Door* where Hugh Hefner's three twentysomething playmate girlfriends each had her own pink bedroom for the nights that Hugh was too tired to take his Viagra. Nala's bedroom had pink walls, a big flat-screen TV, a Hello Kitty bedspread, a pink princess phone, and tons of photos of just Nala and her girlfriends looking their best on a night out, but not one photo of her husband or her kids.

By 7:40 I said, "Nala, we were supposed to be at the restaurant ten minutes ago." She said, "All right, let me just decide on what corset to wear. She chose one with hot-pink roses on it and I had to lace her back up. I felt like I was a lady-in-waiting for Marie Antoinette. She then proceeded to put on a fake ponytail and fake eyelashes, and placed her lip gloss in her crystal-encrusted Hello Kitty clutch. Just as we were about to leave, she said, "Shit, I need money. Daddy, Daddy, I need money." She walked into her husband's bedroom and he met us near the door with a wad of cash.

"How much do you need?"

"A lot. I want to treat the girls," she said.

"No, you don't have to do that," I said.

She brushed me off and took three hundred-dollar bills. We were going to eat Mexican food, where even the steak wasn't more than sixteen, and chips were two bucks.

At the restaurant Nala was very sweet to Liz and Tara, but they were a little put off when she talked about her dream to remarry her husband at the Hello Kitty headquarters in Japan. She ordered a triple Patrón strawberry margarita. First of all, who puts Patrón in a strawberry margarita and then makes it a triple? When her drink arrived, she took one sip of it and asked the waiter for another shot of silver Patrón. I swear I could smell the Patrón through the blended strawberries. Before I realized that Nala hadn't had one bite of her chicken tostada, she ordered another four-shot silver Patrón strawberry margarita. Liz and Tara didn't seem to mind. They enjoyed hearing about the grotto at the Playboy mansion and were fascinated by Nala's mention of having an IQ of 175. I never really understood how IQs worked, but this would be like if Stephen Hawking had a baby with Einstein. It apparently doesn't help with how well you handle your alcohol, because Nala was getting bombed. She kept saying, "I'm drinking my dinner tonight."

As the night went on, Nala started making googly eyes at a man who had to be well into his seventies sitting alone at the table across from us. After a few minutes of this, she went over and joined him. Tara and Liz were ready to call it a night, so I went over to Nala and the senior citizen and told her as much. Nala introduced me to him and I shook his liver-spotted hand. Just then the waiter came to me with the bill. Nala leaped up and grabbed it from my hand, saying, "No, no, no." Then she coyly handed it to the old man and said, "Didn't you say you were going to get this, Daddy?" I was shocked, not that she now had two daddies, but that this brand-new daddy, without a word, *actually* put his card down and handed the bill back to the waiter. After the bill was paid, Nala got up from the old man's table and sat back down at our table, totally ignoring him while calling someone on her Hello Kitty–bedazzled cell phone. She put it on speaker and before the person picked up she asked us, "Who is up for going to Jack Nicholson's house tonight? He should be back from the Lakers game by now." Before any of us could answer we heard a man's voice say, "Hello, Nala." The second I heard it, I imagined Jack Nicholson in his famous black Ray-Ban sunglasses talking on his phone. Nala continued, "Jack, I got some gorgeous, hot young women with me who want to come over tonight. Can you tell Damon at the gate to let us in?" Gorgeous, hot, and young; that was stretching it more than the stretch marks still visible on my stomach and upper thighs. All four of us were over thirty-five, which is still young compared to sixty-seven-year-old Jack, but I doubt he'd be expecting us to drive up in our SUVs equipped with multiple car seats. "Anything for you, Nala," the man said in Jack voice. "OK, Daddy, we'll be there in fifteen minutes." Another daddy? I thought. Who doesn't she call Daddy? Something told me she most likely didn't have a real daddy. Nala then excused herself to go to the restroom. Liz tried to convince us to go, since it was clearly a once-in-a-lifetime chance to meet the star. I argued that he'd be expecting more than preschool conversation from us, which would then lead to an awkward scene of him lounging around watching TV while we tried to convince Nala to leave. I said to Liz, "Besides, what am I supposed to tell her husband if she doesn't leave with me? 'Sorry, after our innocent Mexican food we went to Jack Nicholson's house and Nala decided to take a nap there. See you at school.

By the way, can I list your house?' No, we are not going, and I'm going to insist on taking her home."

When she came back from the restroom, she stopped a waitress and asked for another strawberry margarita with four shots of Patrón. The manager, seeing how wasted Nala was, intervened and said, "I'm sorry, miss, but I think you've had enough." I joined in and said, "Yes, we're leaving, thanks." Then Nala slurred, "Why won't you serve me? Is it because I'm Mexican? That is blatant discrimination, and I'm going to sue." This was the first I was hearing that she was of Mexican descent, and the Mexican manager of the Mexican restaurant was dumbfounded. "Come on, Nala, we're leaving," I said as I grabbed the laces of her corset to help hold her up and pushed her outside. As we walked to the valet I whispered to Tara and Liz not to even mention Jack Nicholson, because I was pretty confident she didn't even remember calling him (assuming, of course, that she even had), and if I could just pour her into my passenger's seat, within a matter of minutes I'd be at her front door and be rid of her.

The next day, Nala called me and told me how she totally threw up into her Hello Kitty toilet and apologized for getting so drunk. I said to her, "Don't worry, it happens to all of us. So when can you, your husband, and I meet so we can go over the comparable sales in your area? I'd love to share all the research I've done for you." I said it in my best Realtor-lady voice.

"Oh, I got the twins' birthday party this weekend, but after that we'll do it. You guys are coming, right?" she asked.

"Yes, of course, we wouldn't miss it," I said. (I still sincerely wanted to be her friend and not just sell her house.) "See you at one on Sunday."

The day of the party, Peter, the kids, and I arrived on time and were greeted by Nala's husband, Ron, and all three of her rotating nannies.

Nala was not there, but as more parents arrived and asked where she was they were told that she was finishing getting ready. Soon we were an hour and a half in and still no Nala. I started to feel sorry for Ron and tried to go along with the idea that it was normal for a mother to miss most of her twins' fourth birthday party that was being held in her living room while she was in her bedroom. The nannies then led us out to the yard, where a large Dora the Explorer piñata was hanging from a tree.

As the first child was being blindfolded to hit the piñata of Dora (let me say here that I don't think it's a great choice for children to see a four-year-old girl hanging from a tree and then bleeding out candy after being beaten with a bat by other children). I looked around and saw an older gentleman whom I recognized as a very successful record producer, a man well into his sixties. I knew this because when I was twenty-six years old, I had been on two very uncomfortable dates with him. Back then, my friend Lily was a practicing gold digger and she forced me to join her and her fifty-seven-year-old ear, nose, and throat doctor boyfriend to a charity event, where I was set up with the record producer. He was at the twins' birthday party alone. I had no interest in telling Peter how I used to date for meals, so I did what any other married mother of three would do: I hid behind the Dora the Explorer piñata and avoided eye contact.

Nala finally emerged from her bedroom looking quite well, wearing a T-shirt that read SHIT HAPPENS and a hot-pink tutu. Just as the nannies were handing out the goody bags. She came up to me and said hi and acted as though she hadn't missed the entire party. I just went along with it and thanked her for inviting us.

That night Nala called to tell me the old record producer, Gary, totally remembered me but didn't want to say anything in front of Peter. She went on to say that she and Gary had been friends since back in the day when they used to date. It was Gary who introduced her to Ron. I had to give both men some props for being so mature and remaining friends all these years. I then attempted to make yet another appointment to discuss the listing of her home by saying, "When shall we meet about getting your home on the market? Right now inventory is low, so your home is sure to get a lot of attention." Nala responded with, "Girl, I know. What's up with Britney Spears these days?" And somehow I ended up with plans to go to a hot new restaurant in Beverly Hills with Nala the following Tuesday night.

Once again, I offered to drive us because I knew I could stay sober enough to get us home. As she was putting on a diamond-encrusted Hello Kitty pendant, Ron came up to her and asked, "Do you need any money?" This time, however, she replied, "No, honey, Gary is paying." What? Gary the old record producer is coming?

I didn't say anything until Nala and I were alone in the car, and then I freaked out. "Nala, why didn't you tell me you *invited* Gary?"

"Because I didn't. He invited us tonight. He said you looked great at the party and really wanted to have dinner."

Well, this was going to be awkward. What would we even talk about? What's happened in the world since 1997 when we saw each other last or if he's had any hips replaced.

"It will be fun and he'll pay for everything," she said.

I replied, "But I'm married and I own a home and have a job and a savings account. I don't need to go out with men I'm not interested in anymore just to get fed. That is the main benefit of being thirty-five and not twenty-six." But Nala just laughed and reapplied her lip liner in my vanity mirror.

When we got to the restaurant, Gary and a young guy around twenty-five were already seated at our table of four. Before we could even sit down, Nala ordered a strawberry daiquiri with only one extra shot of rum. Encouraged by this unexpected sign of restraint, I tried to be optimistic about the evening ahead. But by the time the appetizers arrived Nala was getting drunk and very argumentative with Gary. I thought longingly about the bottle of Chardonnay I could be drinking on my couch, but started asking the twenty-five-year-old guy a bunch of questions. It turned out he was an actor and a Scientologist. Well, at least now I could finally get some answers about Suri Cruise and figure out what makes that little fashionista tick. Somewhere in between him answering questions about L. Ron Hubbard, the idea of a silent birth, and Suri's innate talent for choosing fabrics, I realized that Nala had been in the bathroom for an awfully long time.

Gary told me more than a few times how great I looked, and I told him I was happily married. Soon a waitress gently tapped me on the shoulder and said, "Your friend has been in the bathroom for a really long time and it is the only women's room available. Could you please check on her?"

"Yes, of course," I said, and I excused myself. As I got up to the second floor of the restaurant where the restrooms were, I saw at least six irritated women waiting in line. I don't know why a big restaurant like that one had only one toilet for the women, but it did. I knocked on the door and said, "Nala, it's me, Heather, open up."

"I'll be right out," she said. Nala then opened the door and the stench of regurgitated strawberries and rum was so overwhelming, I almost puked myself. As we headed down the stairs I heard a woman say to another, "Disgusting. We need a janitor in here, stat."

When we were at the valet, Nala said to me, "Gary is going to take me home." At that point I didn't try to fight it. I just wanted to get home to my real husband.

The next day Nala called me and apologized for getting so drunk. "I don't understand. First the Mexican restaurant and then last night. What is going on?" I asked with concern.

"Well, I'm an alcoholic. I thought you knew that," she said matter-of-factly.

That night when I went to bed I started adding up the pros and cons of our friendship. The pros were her amazing Hello Kitty collection, which my stepdaughter, Mackenzie, who was eight years old at the time, was a huge fan of. And then there was that damned house that I was salivating to list and get a commission to refinance our roof. Gosh, I thought, maybe we could even get a solar one. People are shocked by the fact that I'm actually green and that I mulch. The other pro was more for Peter, and I felt it would be a great New Year's Eve gift for him. Nala had said she could get us both invited to the Playboy mansion for their annual ball. Still, we had been warned it wasn't like the good old days. Nala's husband, Ron, told us, "Got to tell you about something just in case you're thinking of it. There are lots of security cameras throughout the mansion now, so you can't just sneak off to a room with another couple and do your business like Nala likes to do."

Ugh. I am grossed out by swingers because the only ones ever featured on documentaries about the subject are old hipsters with aging balls. I simply would never want to join that foursome. Also, what if you were to see them in the drop-off lane at school? How could you admit that you still had their thong and their casserole dish that they left behind the night before? "The four of us have to do it again. I really enjoyed having your husband's penis up my ass."

But back to my friendship with Nala, there was more than just that one negative. In fact, I started to make a list and found myself jotting things down like a court reporter at Michael Jackson's wrongful-death trial with Dr. Conrad Murray

My just-slutty-enough-for-a-mother-
of-three Halloween costume with my
family.

and all the reasons that he should never be allowed to practice medicine again.

Two things came back to me from other mothers who
had met Nala at a Halloween slash Drake's birthday party I
threw. One was while we were all trick-or-treating, an older
woman who lives on our street said to Nala, who was dressed
like a colorful and sexy Carmen Miranda (she had bought her
costume at Trashy Lingerie), "Oh, don't you look spiffy!"

Nala quickly responded, "Did you just call me a spic, ho?
Because I'll go real Mexican on your ass."

Back at the house, my other friend was horrified when
her three-year-old picked up what she thought was a candy

from a Pez dispenser. Nala reached over and said, "Oh no, no, no, baby girl. This is one of my Oxycontins. This is my kind of candy."

And then there was my own list of her past activities that I didn't quite admire in a friend. At thirty-five, if I'm going to be cleaning up puke, it's going to be my own children's, not an aging Playmate's. So I told Peter I needed an out with this friendship. I told him to screen her calls and hoped she would get the message.

For a year she didn't get it, and I would text her back with one-sentence answers explaining how busy I was. Unless I was Ryan Seacrest juggling seventeen shows and a radio gig, did she really think I was that busy? Meanwhile, throughout the year I would frequently drive by her house to make sure that there wasn't a For Sale sign on her lawn. In my Realtor blood, I knew if that one went on the market it would kill pieces of my heart.

A week before the next Halloween, Nala texted me that she'd dropped off a gift and balloons for Drake for his birthday and asked if we'd be celebrating the occasion like we did last year. I was stumped. She just really didn't get it. I texted back, "No, we're not having a party this year, I'm just too busy."

Nala texted back, "Oh well, we enjoyed trick or treating in your neighborhood last year so much, the kids want to go back so we'll see you on your street on Halloween night! Xo, Nala."

Shit. I was having a party, and she would see it. How could I explain myself to her? I finally manned-up and decided to tell her the truth. What can I say? Thank God for texting, or else I'd have had to actually call. I sent her a message stating, "I don't think it's a good idea that you trick-or-treat in my neighborhood because you accused my elderly neighbor of calling you a spic which she did not, and also your grown-up 'candy' might get mixed up with the Sweet Tarts."

I felt pretty good about my honesty and the whole situation until I received her text and read "I just got done talking to Ron that we finally wanted to list our house November first with you. But I guess we'll have to go with Stephanie Marks from Coldwell Banker. Obviously you're just too busy to give us the attention that our property needs." Upon seeing this message I decided to do the Christian thing: I wished Nala the best and prayed that Stephanie Marks wasn't allergic to strawberry margaritas or cats that resemble Hello Kitty.

7

ONE NIPPLE OUT THE DOOR

The plan was always for me to be a breastfeeding mother, and while I was pregnant with my first son, Drake, I took all the prenatal classes including a special one on how to breastfeed. My mother had breastfed all of her children except for me. A week after I was born, my mom insisted on driving her carpool days because, in her words, "I didn't want to owe anyone anything." She was so exhausted that she fell asleep at the wheel and crashed the car. Thank God all the kids were fine; however my brother's hamster died, which wasn't that tragic since no one even knew he had a pet. My mother's nose was broken and she had to spend time in the hospital and her milk dried up, so I was only breastfed for that one week.

As I pushed Drake out, the first thing the doctor said was, "Oh we got a cone head on our hands, get the cap before she sees him." But it was too late. I saw his little scrunched-up face crying and his pointy head, due to being pushed out of my obviously super-tiny and extremely tight vagina. I only bring this up because I'm sick of everyone thinking that those of us who give birth the traditional way have big vaginas compared to their C-section sisters. The nurse put a little cap on him and Drake's head was a normal shape by the next day. I put him on my breasts constantly for the next forty-eight hours and it would soothe him for a little, but he kept crying. He had lost six ounces because he wasn't getting any milk in him, and he was very cranky. The La Leche League, a group of women who help mothers with breastfeeding, came to see me and told me they were concerned that Drake wasn't getting enough milk and sent me home with an electric machine to pump my breasts. About two weeks before I gave birth to Drake, I was watching *Oprah*. The episode was about how for the first time ever mothers were going to talk about how they hated being mothers. I watched and listened intently and I found the common denominator that made these women so miserable was that they all had very difficult and painful breastfeeding experiences.

That night we put the machine on both my huge nipples at the same time so we could fill a bottle with my milk and see if Drake would at least take a bottle, but after pumping for ten minutes, nothing came out and I was crying in excruciating pain. Peter kept asking if we could just give him one of the Similac bottles that the hospital had given us for free, but I cried, "No, then he'll never want my boob because it won't taste the same." Finally after a few more hours of him crying (and by him I mean Peter), I gave in and said, "OK, give me the bottle of Similac. Let me try." The minute Drake's lips touched the bottle's artificial nipple, he was sucking like crazy. I had to pull it away so he could digest it. It was as if he'd just been released from Auschwitz, he was so famished.

That night, my mother-in-law, who was helping us, woke me up at two a.m. and said, "Drake is hungry, do you want to try to breastfeed him again?" I said, "No, please give him the bottle." And I then went back to sleep. It was such a great feeling knowing that he had four ounces, or two ounces, or whatever. I just loved knowing that he was eating. I know the Le Leche League will hate me for giving up after only three days, but I believe it is still a mother's choice, and I don't believe that a child is so much better off drinking breast milk

Here is the most inappropriate, odd pregnancy photo ever. My art-photographer friend, Dick Sanders, took it and he talked me into showing areola. P.S. PETA: don't freak out— the fur is fake. *(©Dick Sanders)*

than one of the wonderful formulas out there. That's like me insisting that all margaritas be made with Patrón tequila. Is that really fair to Jose Cuervo?

I called my mom the next day and said, "I made a decision. Drake is going to be bottle fed, and I don't want to hear any more about it. He is doing great." My mom assured me that she didn't care and whatever I wanted was fine. Let me add, here, that despite being the only one of five children not breastfed, I am the closest to my mother and the tallest of the three girls.

A week later, I was at the gas station pumping my gas and on the other side of the pump was a real-estate agent from my mother's office. She said, "How is the baby? I heard the breastfeeding wasn't for you." I got that a lot. Even the checker at our grocery store knew my entire breastfeeding story. Apparently, my mom was buying formula for her house and felt the need to explain. I know women get shit for whipping out a tit in public, but I got just as much, if not more, shit for whipping out a can of formula instead. Still, for our family it really worked. I would have felt so guilty if my son had gas and was in pain because I chose to eat a spicy enchilada one night. When I gave birth to my second son, Brandon, I told the nurses before he was even born that I was not breastfeeding. The first morning after I woke up in the hospital I called to the nursery to have them send me Brandon and the nurse said, "We just fed him and he's sleeping. Do you want to rest and we'll bring him to you when he wakes?" It was wonderful to relax with my cranberry juice, icy maxi pad, and a TV remote all to myself. Besides, this way Peter could do the five-a.m. feedings, which he did for both boys. When I look back at my marriage, those five-a.m. feedings are some of the fondest memories I have of Peter as a husband. Otherwise, it's just a lot of Peter snoring, farting, and clearing out his throat.

I try not to judge when women choose to breastfeed past one year. If that is what they want to do, so be it. I mean, I don't think it should happen during a soccer game right after your son scores a goal and wants a sip off your num-nums, but if it goes to two or even three years old, I really don't think it is anyone's business.

Since I wasn't breastfeeding, I tried to make up for the "bonding" that I was told I was missing out on in other ways, like enlisting a baby masseuse. I saw a flyer that read "Give your infant the ultimate gift of relaxation and bonding with a baby masseuse expert." Perfect, I thought. I love massages, and the flyer said it would help the baby sleep and with digestion, which the Le Leche League claimed my baby might struggle with without my sacred breast milk. I called the woman whose number was listed on the flyer and when she answered she spoke so softly to me on the phone, I could barely hear her. She spoke like the Duggar mother on TLC's *19 Kids and Counting.* Michelle Duggar is so softspoken and so slow in her speech, it is astounding that she has nineteen kids. But maybe that is because she never really has to scold them, because each older child is assigned to raise a younger child. No wonder the parents still have time to bone and get pregnant. Essentially, she has ten nannies working for her. I tried to explain to Peter that the baby masseuse was coming over. To keep the peace, I lied and said the first consultation was free. It actually cost fifty dollars a session, which is not terrible. A massage for a regular-size adult would be twice that amount.

The baby masseuse, Lawson, arrived that afternoon wearing all pastels, with a tie-dye sarong wrapped around her flowing pants, which is not the most flattering look because it's just a lot of extra material. But she wasn't a model, she was a baby masseuse. We went into my family room and she told me to lay Drake down on a blanket facing me while she did the same with a baby doll she brought. Then she said, "Now, before you touch your son you need to respect him and you do that by always asking 'May I touch you?'" First of all, this was already the worst massage because Lawson had no intention of even touching my baby. But I did as I was told and softly asked, "May I touch you?" Since Drake was just a few months old, he just stared at me, confused. I began to touch him anyway and followed Lawson's instruction as she showed me where to rub him on her doll. Peter came home and just gave me his classic "Are you fucking kidding me?" look. I introduced him to the baby masseuse and she whispered back, "Nice to meet you, but we're in session and the client still has twenty minutes left."

I asked Lawson how she got involved in baby massage and she explained it was just one among many of her successful business ventures, including making her own potpourri and studying to be a hypnotist. Drake really didn't seem that into it as I was rubbing him. I began to worry he might not leave a decent tip, so I cut the session short and told Lawson I'd be in touch when Drake had a stressful day and really needed a

Swedish deep-tissue combo. I can understand getting a massage for your dog, but getting one for your infant seems a little extravagant, even for L.A.

Once when I was out with Drake, in an elevator an older woman looked down at him in the stroller with his little fat cheeks and said, "Now that is a breastfed baby if I've ever seen one." I responded, "Yes, he is! My nipples are chapped and bleeding and my breasts are misshapen but it's all worth it for my baby. Thanks for noticing what good health he is in." I'll admit that once at an outdoor café I covered myself with a receiving blanket and fed Drake with a bottle under it so it would appear like I was breastfeeding to avoid being judged by the other mothers whose babies were under their shirts. Hey, it is no secret that breastfeeding screws up your tits. I have a few friends who breastfed and now would really like their breasts done. One girlfriend in particular is so miserable in her marriage that if she got a boob job, she'd be one nipple out the door.

Regarding the chatter about how a breastfed baby has a stronger immune system, I'd say you haven't met Drake. Drake is nine, and to this day he has never had a fever, or an earache, or been on antibiotics. I know, I find it weird too. Especially one night, when I was channel surfing and came across the classic 1976 horror movie *The Omen,* where a wealthy couple starts to believe their five-year-old son might be the antichrist. At one point the mother says, "Don't you find it strange that Damien has never been sick, never even had a fever?" Oh my God, I thought, nearly sputtering out my mouthful of wine, could Drake be the antichrist? I'd be lying if I said I didn't comb his scalp and search for the numbers 666 written on his skull. However, I'm happy to report I have yet to find those numerals, or any tiny white eggs. Although, that is mostly because my husband doesn't wash their hair very often and lice are only attracted to clean hair. It's one positive way for me to look at Peter's parenting skills and the kids' lack of hygiene. I dispensed this theory when I had to defend Drake against one mother who was trying to pin my son as Patient Zero for the great lice outbreak of 2008.

8

GOOD HELP IS HARD TO FIND

When I would take Drake as a baby to the park, all the other kids had their Spanish nannies and they would all ask for *agua* and Drake would just ask for water. He seemed so much less sophisticated. So with Brandon I was feeling pretty good about myself for hiring a Spanish speaking nanny. I thought Brandon could grow up bilingual. Juanita worked for us a couple of days a week, taking care of Brandon and cleaning the house. In the beginning the house was spotless and she would even cook for us. When I started working for *Chelsea Lately* full-time, we hired her to work five days a week. Juanita was great. She always had a smile on her face, despite the fact that the baby daddy of her three children left her for her older sister. Her life was like a Telemundo soap opera.

About a year in, things started to change a little with Juanita's attitude. She wasn't supposed to drive the kids around, but she started to do her personal errands during the workday with our children in tow. I found out because Drake told me how much he loved the 99-cent store, and we had never been there before. He also kept asking for Taco Bell. Her housework was becoming more and more lax. And she started putting my clothes in Mackenzie's closet. When I brought it up to her, she said, "Oh, Miss Heather, it was so little I thought it was for a young girl, not a mother of three. Sorry." I thought it was a pretty passive-aggressive move on her part. What's so wrong with a married mother in her late thirties wearing a cropped top?

One afternoon, I came home early only to discover that she had thrown a fiesta in our backyard with all the other Mexican nannies and the kids they watched. They were all enjoying the Slip 'N Slide, and Los Lobos' music was playing on the outdoor speakers so loudly that all the neighbors thought that a construction crew was building an addition onto our house.

After that incident, I told her I didn't want her driving the kids around and that she couldn't have other nannies and their children over because it was a liability if we weren't there.

Things got even more unsettling when I bought my dad a hundred-dollar gift card at Target for his birthday. When I went to find it, I couldn't locate it in my desk drawer. I scoured the house and I told myself, once again, Heather, you are so disorganized. Now you've actually lost something of value. In the back of my mind, I prayed, *Oh, God, please do not tell me that Juanita stole it.*

A week later, Peter and I were going out to dinner and Juanita was watching the kids. I had left a wallet with a hundred-dollar bill in my drawer. The next morning on my way to work, I went to pay for my Starbucks coffee and noticed that the hundred was gone. Shit, I thought, now I don't have cash for the Chinese chicken salad at the food truck. But more important, I had my confirmation that Juanita had taken the money and the cash card. I told Peter about the two missing items, and he said, "All right, but I'm not a hundred percent convinced, because you lose stuff all of the time." He was intrigued enough to buy some little spy cameras, which we set up in his office, where the cash is kept.

At that point, I was scared of her getting caught and us having to fire her, because I didn't want to find a new person. Wasn't there some sort of nanny rehabilitation program out there? I called my lawyer sister, Shannon, and asked her whether she thought it was wise that I tell Juanita about Peter's sting operation. She said, "Heather, that would be an obstruction of justice." Hmm, I thought. That sounded serious, coming from my sister, so I kept my lips sealed.

That Monday, the cameras were rolling and Peter and I left Juanita at 8:30 a.m. and I went off to work. At 4:35 that afternoon, Peter called me from the house and he said, "Oh my God, I'm shaking, I am shaking right now. I can't believe what I just saw. Juanita just left, so I checked the videos from the security cameras and at 8:41 a.m. it shows Juanita walking into my office while talking on the cell phone. She went straight to the money drawer, lifted up the notepads that cover it, counted out the $720 in cash that was there and took $260 of it and shoved the rest back under the notepad. I'm so surprised. I never said this to you, but there were times over the last six months when I thought I had more cash in the drawer. You're going to die when you see the video."

As I was driving home, I started to reflect on my relationship with Juanita. She had gotten acrylic French-tipped nails that she was able to keep up with weekly manicure visits, which I thought was strange considering she was supposed to be scrubbing toilets, doing dishes, and changing diapers. She had also had professional tooth bleaching done and gotten hair extensions. She was becoming the Sofia Vergara of maids.

I arrived home and went straight to Peter's home office. When Peter showed me the surveillance video that confirmed Juanita was stealing, I felt like I was with Chris Hansen on *Dateline*: "To Catch a Domestic Thief" episode. Her casualness really struck me and I became upset to think how she not only looked after the boys but that she was part of our family. I'd never had someone betray me like this. I had never even had a boyfriend cheat on me, so this was heartbreaking.

I couldn't fire her, as I knew she would cry and tell me how her children now call her sister, Mommy, instead of Aunt, since her sister was the one sleeping with her baby daddy. I simply couldn't deal with the drama, so I asked Peter to do it. When Juanita came to work the next day he said to her cheerfully, "Oh, come here, I want to show you something on my computer."

As she watched, Juanita started to cry and said, "No, no, Mr. Peter, I was just borrowing the money. I was going to return it on my payday." She was acting just like the guys on "To Catch a Predator" when confronted by Chris and his camera crew presenting a predator with the e-mails he wrote a thirteen-year-old virgin: "Oh, I never planned on sleeping with her. She e-mailed me that she was hungry so I just wanted to bring the Happy Meal over to her. The Mike's Hard Lemonade is just for me. And the condoms, um, well, those are for us to make water balloons because she wrote me that she wanted to have a pool party." Unlike *Dateline,* we didn't call the cops, so they didn't come out of the bushes and tackle Juanita on our front lawn. We went about it in a more dignified manner. Peter just told her that she had to leave. She asked if she could call me, probably to beg for her job knowing I'm a sap, but Peter said no.

The next night, we went out to dinner for Liz's birthday. At the dinner Kris Jenner and Kourtney Kardashian were seated next to me. I told them, "I just had the most horrible thing happen with my nanny." Kris immediately asked while smiling, "Oh, did you find out she had been stealing from you?" I was surprised by how quickly she guessed it. I filled them in on more of the story and Kourtney said, "Oh my gosh, Mom, you were so oblivious that Margarita was stealing from us, but you wouldn't fire her because you didn't want to be without help." Kourtney went on to say, "When my brother, Robert, was ten, all his clothes kept going missing. And then, Mom, you would just let him spend the night at Margarita's house in downtown L.A." Kris chimed in,

"Well, Margarita had two sons right around Robert's age." Kourtney said, "Right, and when he returned he said, 'Mom, José and Manny have all the same clothes that I have. You know, the ones I can't find anymore, like the khakis and the alligator shirts." Kris said, "Well, she was so good with Kendall and Kylie, I didn't want to make a big deal out of it. But then one day, I bought a big box of Equal sweetener from Costco, and the next day, I found a bag filled with the Equal packets in my bushes. So I put two and two together and realized she forgot to put the bag of Equal in her car. She would take half of my Costco purchases so I wouldn't ever notice. Oh, was I fooled. But that was the final straw, the Equals, and I held up the bag and asked adamantly, 'Are you forgetting something, Margarita? I didn't know you loved artificial sweetener so much?' "

A year later, my sister Shannon was bragging about the amazing maid she had and how she would clean her house at the speed of light and organize all her closets. Shannon couldn't believe how much extra space she had in her dresser drawers. Imagine Shannon's shock when her neighbor told her she was at the local swap meet and saw Shannon's maid, Carlita, working a booth selling name-brand children's and women's clothing and that upon further inspection she discovered Shannon's son Matthew's name was written on several of the tags inside the shirts. Shannon, like me, wussed out, and told her maid she was putting her children in full-time day care, instead of firing her. She later discovered Carlita was arrested for selling and using speed. No wonder she was able to clean Shannon's house so fast.

When the news broke about our former California governor Arnold Schwarzenegger's love child whom he fathered with his and Maria Shriver's housekeeper of almost twenty years, I empathized so much with Maria. I had never felt more deceived than when Juanita stole money from us. Imagine if she had stolen my husband's sperm and given birth to his child, and we had to pay child support. Juanita only got some new nails and shining teeth out of me, but poor Maria landed a stepson.

But you know Maria. She is such a positive person, I'm confident she can make something good of this. She has written bestselling children's books titled *What's Heaven?* and *What's Happening to Grandpa?* so now she can write, *What's the Reason Our Maid's Son Looks Like Our Dad?*

I know this story is the epitome of "White Girl Problems." So you'll be happy to know I'm starting a grassroots charity called "Vans of Love," where vans could provide transportation for domestics from the Boulevard bus stop to their home of employment for middle-class L.A. families who cannot afford to have live-in help. I think it would be perfect for when I'm working for Donald Trump on *The Celebrity Apprentice* and need a designated charity. Donald of all people would be sensitive to the needs of those Americans whose homes don't come equipped with maid's quarters.

9

THEY TRIED TO MAKE ME GO TO REHAB

I was opening for Chelsea a few years ago at the Hard Rock Hotel and Casino in Las Vegas. I decided to bring the boys, since Vegas is so close and I never get to bring the kids on the road. We arrived on Saturday, and I did my act that night. The next morning I encouraged Peter to go golfing with his brother, who lived in Las Vegas, while I enjoyed a day at the pool with the boys. From the moment we arrived, the boys had been eyeing the huge pool and waterslide that they could see from our room. At eleven a.m. we headed to the pool area, and I was surprised to see all the security involved for just taking a dip in the pool. They checked our bags and my sons' sippy cups to make sure it was apple juice and not alcohol. A nice security guard advised me to perhaps leave by two. I thought, Isn't that sweet, he's worried about my boys getting too much sun.

We put our stuff on some lounge chairs and lotioned up. At first the boys (aged six and three at the time) complained about the loud noise coming from the DJ spinning techno beats, but they forgot about it as soon as they got to the slide. Brandon was psyched because no lifeguard was there to tell him he was too short to go on the ride. At around one, Chelsea came to the pool, and my kids, who adore her, went over and asked if she would go down the slide with them. She looked horrified and said, "Oh, kids, I would, but I'm afraid I'll get pregnant. I don't want to give birth to a baby that craves Ed Hardy."

I started to notice that the pool area was getting more crowded, but with no other kids. I was seeing *Jersey Shore* types. Every guy was super-tanned, roided-out, and had greasy Guido hair. The women were even more memorable. It's not like they were Miss Americas in the bathing-suit competition. They were the type to wear super-tiny triangle tops that just covered the nipple and thong bikini bottoms, paired with clear strappy platform heels. They reminded me of those Bratz dolls that Mackenzie used to play with. They come in a box with huge glossy lips and big hair, wearing crop tops, a pleather miniskirt, and no underwear so they can get in the club for free. Basically, they're Barbie's slutty second cousin who comes to visit her in college and does Barbie's boyfriend, Ken, in her dorm room while Barbie is at her Poli Sci 101 class. There were so many tattoos of hearts and butterflies and inspirational sayings written appropriately just under their tits. We were becoming outnumbered.

The boys couldn't have cared less, because they had the waterslide all to themselves. Strippers tend to avoid waterslides, since their high heels could get caught in the twists and turns, and their hair extensions would frizz up if they got wet.

At one point, Brandon needed to use the restroom, which was located by the second pool near where the party was really happening. People were dancing and grinding like it was a nightclub at a pool. I picked Brandon up on my hip so that I could hold him. As we made our way, we passed plenty of women drinking Mojitos out of penis-shaped straws. Suddenly, I noticed that the men were looking at me. I know I'm pretty, but I definitely couldn't compare to these types of Vegas showgirls. I figured they must have come to see my stand-up act the night before. Right as we got to the bathroom, some kind girl exclaimed to me, "Oh my God, the top of your bathing suit . . ." I looked down and saw that Brandon had mistakenly pulled down my top while he was holding on to me, completely exposing my boob. I immediately repositioned myself to stop my nipple from winking at the world and took him into the bathroom. As we walked back toward our lounge chairs, I finally noticed the signs that said 21 AND OVER ONLY, STRICTLY ENFORCED. It was definitely past two in the afternoon. When we got back to our area, I went to the bar to get the boys two Sprites. The only option was to get the forty-eight-ounce sipper with Sprite minus the vodka, which I still had to pay for. Chelsea and her entourage were now in a cabana. Chelsea said, "Heather, are you kidding me? It's time for you to leave and let the grown-ups play. This isn't *Kids Gone Wild*." I said, "I'm not as inappropriate as you may think. I've been trying to get them to leave but they just keep saying, 'Please, Mom, just one more time down the slide.'"

Chelsea said, "You mean the Hepatitis C slide? Heather, aren't you the mother? If you stay another ten minutes, they are going to see something that will scar them for life."

I took Chelsea's advice and gathered up my family. We left the pool area and the party, which was called "Rehab."

Brandon on what my colleagues referred
to as the Hepatitis C slide.

When I got back to work on Monday, everyone was making fun of me for bringing my kids to the pool. They were threatening to call Child Protective Services and have my children removed from my care. Brad Wollack, one of my fellow writers, said to me, "Heather, don't you know they have paramedics on hand for when people OD, or pass out from alcohol poisoning? I decided to Google Hard Rock Hotel and Rehab and discovered something that read: "Everyone knows [except for me] that some of the best partying in Las Vegas happens during the daytime poolside. And the ultimate Vegas pool party? The Hard Rock Hotel invented it with Rehab. The once intimate poolside party has grown into a destination with weekend revelers in the thousands. Get ready for Rock Star Lemonades, world-famous DJs, celebrity guests, and the best time you'll have in Vegas. The beautiful, the tattooed, the rich, the famous, large and small, everyone gets down on Rehab Sunday."

Then it hit me. When they said large and small I don't think they meant six- and three-year-old boys.

I hoped that would be the last time I would ever take my sons to rehab. However, I would like to go to rehab one day, not for any problem I have but just to go to Promises in Malibu for a thirty-day stint paid for by insurance. I could enjoy days of yoga and journaling, and going to group therapy to talk about myself. I wouldn't wear makeup and would let my hair dry naturally so by the time I left I'd be glowing and my hair would shine like a L'Oréal commercial from not having heat on it for weeks. When not telling stories about myself I'd offer up my motherly advice to the real addicts. I'd say things like "It's not that your mom had a favorite, it's just that their personality traits are more evident in one child over another and therefore it is easier for them to relate to and parent that child versus the one who is drinking and doing drugs. Did you ever think your sister might have been more enjoyable to take shopping because she wasn't shooting up heroin in the dressing room?" I'm sorry, but in my research of watching *Celebrity Rehab* and *Sober House* on VH1, I think parents get blamed a little too much.

On *Chelsea Lately,* I used to do a wicked Amy Winehouse

impersonation. After she died, I thought, What a waste of my talents. It was such a good wig and now I had to just hang it in my office to remember Amy. I got many condolence Facebook postings and tweets, and for a moment I empathized with what Amy had gone through.

I performed again in Vegas recently, and the boys asked if they could go to the cool place with the slide called Rehab. But I said, "No. No. No."

10

WILD WORLD

Wild World USA is an amusement park in Valencia, California, and approximately a forty-five-minute drive from our house in Woodland Hills. When I was growing up, my parents preferred Wild World over Disneyland since it was closer. Because my parents worked every day selling residential real estate, at the beginning of my summer vacation, my dad would open his rugged calendar, pick out one day, and write "Wild World" on it in red pen—not pencil like everything else. That meant no matter what, they would not make appointments on that chosen day. My mom, my dad, Shannon, and I would spend the entire day riding roller coasters until the park closed.

Summer in Valencia, California, is the closest I will ever get to hell (I'm praying). An average afternoon in July can get as high as 115 degrees. But not to worry—after waiting in line for two hours and fifteen minutes, you can get sprinkled with ten drops of cool water as the log that you are sitting in flies down a rinky-dink river, completing your fifty-four seconds of bliss.

As a kid, I could barely sleep the night before our trip to Wild World. I remember having my pink shorts and matching halter top all laid out along with my clear jelly flats so that if they got wet on the Wet 'n' Wonderful—the best of the water rides—they'd dry quickly, unlike the pairs of sneakers my amateur sibling was wearing. I planned on wearing a ponytail and hot-pink visor. I put my Chapstick, sunscreen, and some money in a small purse that I'd wear diagonally across my chest, so there was no way it could fall off while I was going 110 miles per hour upside down on the Rebellion.

I woke up at eight a.m. and quickly ran to Shannon's room. I was nine, and Shannon was eleven. After waking her up, I went into my parents' room and said cheerfully, "Mom, Dad, wake up! The park opens at ten." Then I heard my mom moan, "Oh, Bob, I don't feel good." My heart fell. *She has to get better.* I prayed three Hail Marys. This was the one day I'd been counting down the days, the hours, the minutes, and the seconds for to arrive. I knew how many active listings my parents had, so if it wasn't going to be that day, it wouldn't be until the next *year* that we could go again. I guess Shannon and I laid enough guilt on my mom, because she got dressed and we were on the freeway to Wild World within an hour. Why she didn't just suggest that she stay home and make my dad go, I don't understand, but I guess she felt like I do now. As a guilty working mom she really wanted to spend the day with us having fun and not miss out on the memory. Within minutes of entering the gates my mom said, "Bob, I need to sit down." Next thing we knew, she was lying down on a bed in the Wild World hospital, but she insisted that we leave her and enjoy ourselves, so the three of us were off to wait in the lines. Every few hours we'd go by to check on her and the nurse would say she was fine, but sleeping. At around eleven thirty p.m. we took our last ride (you can see we were serious about our time at the park, sick mom and all). We had the nurse wake Mom up when it was time to go. My mom said she never felt better and it was one of the best days she'd had in the past decade. As a mom, I totally get it now. She was sick and needed to sleep, but if she had stayed home, she would have felt guilty about resting. At the Wild World hospital, however, she had found her happy place. If only I had caught on a little quicker.

It's very rare that I am alone. But when I'm on the road performing stand-up and I don't have anything to do the next morning, I just want to sleep. Sometimes I get so tired I fantasize about being admitted to the hospital and being treated for exhaustion, Mariah Carey–style. Like when I have what I like to call a "sleep party." It's a party where only I am invited, and it's amazing. First I pee several times so I don't wake up in the middle of the night, then I turn off my phone, and finally I take two Advil PMs. Sometimes they make me thirsty, so I make sure I have a glass of water by my bed. I dress in warm pajamas with socks, and I keep a sleep mask by my bed in case I need to put it on in the morning just to get a few more hours in. My record is ten and a half hours. The joy I feel when I wake up and count how many hours I slept is a feeling of amazing accomplishment. It's the same jubilation I believe Neil Armstrong felt when he walked on the moon.

From that point on, my mom never joined us again at Wild World. She didn't enjoy the scary rides anyway, and I think she came to that place of "Let's not, and say I did." We didn't mind, just as long as *we* were going.

Once in line for the Swashbuckler, a pirate ship that swings really high from side to side, some boys around twelve years old were cutting in line by running under the iron bars to the next row when my dad, the Marine, reached down and grabbed one of the boys by his collar and lifted him in the air and said, "What the hell do you think you're doing?" The kid was speechless and my dad continued. "All of you get to the back of the line, or I'll call for security and have you little shits thrown out of here." The boy called to his friends, who were witnessing what was happening, and said, "Come on, guys, this ride is lame anyway." And the three of them bolted as other parents cheered and shook my dad's hand. That day, I said to myself, "One day I'm going to be rich enough to rent out Wild World for my birthday and I won't have to wait in line for any ride all day long. Could anything be greater than that?"

But I felt I always made the most of the hour-long waits to get on the rides. I loved to people-watch and kept myself busy reading all the tattoos of the people ahead of me. I wondered if their mothers were a little less disappointed if their tattoos were religious, or read I ♥ MOM. Yes, your son got a tattoo on his back, but it's of Jesus Christ going to all twelve Stations of the Cross. I'd fantasize about one day having a boyfriend, where I could stick my tongue down his throat for four minutes then walk one foot forward in line, and then he'd stick his tongue down my throat for another four minutes. I think I officially learned how babies were made while in line for the Rebellion. I dreamed that one day in the future a boy would put his hands in the back pockets of my Jordache jeans as I put my palms in his back pockets, and we would walk facing each other like that until we eventually got to the front.

I've still never forgiven my dad for the day he grounded me from going to Wild World ten minutes before my friends came to pick me up because, in his opinion, I did a sloppy job stuffing the envelopes for their real-estate mailer. I hated running out and telling Tara, Liz, and Heather Cross that I couldn't join them. At sixteen, you had to have a fourth person, otherwise one teenage girl would be subjected to sitting next to a possible pedophile on a ride, so I really felt like I let them down. Also, by now we were finally four somewhat cute teenage girls. I was planning on meeting a hot guy to grind on against the metal dividers in line.

My most traumatic Wild World experience occurred when I was about eleven. My dad, my sister, and I planned to go one weekday during our spring break. When you go to Catholic school, they give you the week off after Easter, which is different from the public schools' spring break probably because they didn't want us to socialize with the public-school kids. I remember my dad telling me to call and find

out what Wild World's hours were in case they were different from the summer, but I got distracted with an episode of
Growing Pains and I never phoned. Driving there that morning
my dad accidently missed the off-ramp, and as he was turning around, I was staring at their largest, most popular roller
coaster, the Monster. After several minutes I still hadn't seen
the little train of screaming people go by. I got a pit in my
stomach. Was the ride broken? Oh no! As we drove up my
dad said, "Look, no one is in the parking lot. We must be the
first ones here. Thank God you guys have a different week
off than the public-school kids." And then we saw it. A sign
that read PLEASE ACCEPT OUR APOLOGIES. WILD WORLD WILL BE
CLOSED FROM APRIL 9–15TH. I burst into tears. My dad was so
sweet, he didn't scold me for not calling. In fact, he didn't
even bring it up. Then he suggested going to the beach instead. "But we didn't bring our bathing suits or towels," my
sister and I cried. So instead he got back on the freeway and
drove all the way to Disneyland, in Anaheim, the Taj Mahal of
amusement parks. We didn't get there until one p.m., but we
had the best time ever, and stayed until it closed at ten.

This past Christmas vacation, Peter's sister, Karen, and her
two kids, aged thirteen and fifteen, were coming to visit us
the day after the holiday. We decided to go to Wild World,
because for a group of ten it was only going to be twenty-
seven dollars each—a serious deal. And I was kind of excited,
as I had not been since I was a teenager and was curious to
check out the new rides. The night beforehand, it was very

warm, so we decided to heat up the pool and have some families over. We started drinking around two p.m. After going in the Jacuzzi, drying off, and getting dressed, I was pouring another glass of wine when I noticed Liz's three-year-old son trying to get a ball out of the pool. This made me nervous, so I decided to get the toys out of the pool and put the automatic cover on. I got the ball out successfully; however, when I went to grab the water gun I lost my balance and fell in the pool—fully clothed, with my shoes still on my feet. My wineglass also fell in with me, making the pool one giant wine spritzer. My husband ran over with a camera and I posed while floating in the shallow end still holding my wineglass. Luckily, that convinced me to stop drinking for the night, so I felt fine the next morning for our big day at Wild World. Peter, however, had continued to drink red wine and smoke cigars, and was in horrible shape.

I don't condone my husband smoking cigars. In fact, one night when I was telling Drake his bedtime story—which I'm required to do by Drake every night and it has to be completely made up and cannot have a character named Drake in it or any name that rhymes with Drake—I added how the little boy's teeth got yellow from smoking and he had to smoke cigarettes out of a hole in his neck (yes, I draw from popular Public Service Announcements for inspiration). Drake then replied, "But Daddy smokes."

"No, he doesn't," I snapped back.

"Yes, I've seen him do it with Mikey's dad," he argued.

"Well, those are cigars, but you're right, anything you smoke is bad and Daddy's not going to do it anymore." I didn't want him becoming some pothead, thinking that's OK because it's organic or some other hippie shit. I immediately walked into the bedroom and told Peter, "The kids can't see you smoke cigars anymore. We can't preach what we don't practice. I'm serious, if the kids are around, no cigars."

A couple of weeks later, we were at Liz's house and she had a few families over. At around eight p.m. I started to smell cigar smoke but didn't know where it was coming from because none of the husbands were in the backyard. Then I heard a loud crash. Peter and three other men all well over two hundred pounds each had snuck up into Liz's three-year-old son Ethan's tree house to smoke their cigars so the kids wouldn't see them, and the fragile wood planks in the floor could not hold the weight. Thankfully, no one was too hurt. I tried to make the best out of it and told the boys, "See? Smoking is dangerous and the mommy always finds out if you ever try to hide it like Daddy did."

The morning we left for Wild World, I remembered when my mom was sick all those years ago, and found it in my heart not to push Peter to join us. Instead, I told him to stay home and clean up the backyard, take down the Christmas lights, and do three loads of laundry because that's the kind of cool wife I am. Then my sister-in-law, Karen; mother-in-law, Ginny; and six kids and I were off for a day of fun.

When we drove up, we saw plenty of cars—thousands in fact, so at least I had the comfort of knowing it wasn't closed. However, Wild World doesn't have the little open buses that transport you from the parking lot to the front of the park, so after about five minutes of walking, five-year-old Brandon started whining, "Carry me, carry me, Mommy." I put him on my back but after a few minutes he was feeling really heavy and I thought they should have guys you can hire for the day just to carry your kid around at amusement parks the way you pick someone up outside of a Home Depot to help you move or paint your gate. In our journey from our car to the gate I noticed several teenagers downing what looked to be tequila as they pushed their toddlers in strollers. I could understand why when we got to the top of the hill and saw the large sign prohibiting alcohol consumption.

Next we saw all the metal detectors, which is the first thing you have to walk through before you even purchase tickets to enter the park. A woman ahead of me was stopped by an employee until she pulled up her pant leg and said, "Alcohol monitor." The employee then directed her to a different metal detector, and then he yelled to the crowd, "If you have an alcohol-monitored ankle bracelet, please go through the metal detector that specifies that over here to the right." What a classy crowd.

I had my printout from the Internet that I thought was our ticket into the park, but when I showed it to the Wild World officer, he said what I had was only for our Express Pass and it did not include the park entrance fee. After waiting in that line for twenty minutes I was told that we still had to buy the entrance tickets for either thirty-five dollars a person or twenty-seven dollars a person for a party of ten. I was with Peter's mother and sister, who, like Peter, are both carriers of the cheap gene, so they insisted we buy ten tickets at twenty-seven dollars instead of the eight at thirty-five because it would be ten dollars cheaper and we could sell the other two leftover tickets. It was already twelve thirty and the park closed at eight p.m. This was not the way I wanted to do the amusement park. I didn't want to waste any more time, so I agreed. When I started passing out the tickets I said, "Look, I'm on TV. I can't go scalp two tickets to Wild World. What if I get caught? And worse, what if no one recognizes me while I'm trying to do it? That will be downright humiliating. Let's just go in the park." But Karen convinced me to wait ten minutes while we sent out Kimberly, our nineteen-year-old niece, to sell the tickets. As we sat there waiting for Kimberly to return with the cash, I started to look around at all the teenagers and was in awe of their incredible confidence. Apparently love handles are all the rage for this generation, and if you got them, then flaunt them. Picture them pouring out of a pair of acid-washed skinny jeans and pair it with a T-shirt stating YOU WISH YOU WERE MY BOYFRIEND. All I'm saying is, based on what I witnessed that day, teen anorexia has to be on the decline.

Kimberly returned with two crisp twenties and the swagger of an experienced crack dealer. She said, "No big deal. I told the guy, 'Walk away, roll up the two twenty-dollar bills in the palm of your hand and then come back here in three minutes, shake my hand, and you and your little friend will be on the Rocketeer in no time.'" I was so impressed I said, "All those years of being a latchkey child and watching reruns of *Law & Order* really paid off."

OK, now, where do we get our Express Pass and what is it, exactly? I wondered. We were told to go into a building across the quad to get it. When we entered the Express Pass building, it was extremely stuffy and each person who tried to help us directed us to another room and then another room. In the third room, the most unenthusiastic nineteen-year-old boy greeted us with greasy, dyed-black hair covering one eye and his earlobes as large as saucers because he had those earrings in each one that makes the piercing in the ear a super-large hole so you can see right through it, and the earrings can double as bangle bracelets. He went on to explain, "In order to receive your Express Pass, you need to listen to the brief video explaining how the Express Pass works. If you lose the Express Pass, you will be charged $250 and you must return the pass here fifteen minutes before we close. Does everyone understand?" We all said yes, and the video began. It was a pretty complicated computer that was the size of an old-style pager. In the video it went through all the different levels of the Express Pass. It was so confusing and hot in there that I started to feel claustrophobic. Now it was one p.m. and we had only seven hours left. When the Spanish version concluded we were able to move on to the next room to finally receive our Express Pass devices. We were told, yet again, about the fee if we lost or damaged it, this time by a twenty-something woman with a piercing in her nose and lip, until I finally interrupted, "Yes, we want it! Where do I sign? The day is half over already!"

As soon as I signed the paper, she said, "Please let me draw your attention to all the Express Pass rides that are temporarily closed today. The list was about ten rides long. "What, all of those? Did we even need the Express Pass today?" I questioned the girl with the jewelry face. I'm bothered by these piercings because when you take the hoop out of your nose, it's going to look like you have a massive pore, and the one in the lip must be virtually impossible to maneuver MAC lip liner around. "Probably not, but you can't get your fifty-five dollars per person back now because you signed the consent form."

Well, now we were roughly seven hundred dollars in the hole, had been there over an hour, and had yet to do one fun thing.

Then I knew what I had to do next. I had to have "the talk" with my youngest and smallest child.

I was afraid we were going to have a repeat of what happened at a hotel in Arizona recently with a waterslide where Brandon wasn't tall enough. I was already at the pool and when I saw Peter and the boys walking up to me, I could immediately see Brandon was crying. "What's wrong?" I asked. Drake chimed in, "He's not tall enough to go on the slide. I told him, and he's freaking out." Oh no, the horror known as "little brother syndrome." There is nothing worse than when your big brother can do something but you're told you can't because of your size. I had to try to fix it. "Just come with me," I said as I held Brandon's hand and we began to walk up the steps to the slide. I was hoping that when we got up there the lifeguard wouldn't notice Brandon's lack of height or would be distracted by texting. First I used my fingers to spike up his wet hair into a faux Mohawk to give him a little height and edge, in the hopes it would make him less likely to be fucked with. Then when it got close to our turn to go down the slide,

I told him to stand up tall and then immediately sit down on the slide until the lifeguard cleared him to go. I figured if he was sitting, the lifeguard wouldn't notice how not-tall he was. Brandon did as he was told but the lifeguard took one look at his little legs and said, "Hey buddy, you want to come over here?" As he pointed to the height chart, waiting for Brandon to stand by it, Brandon's chocolate eyes stared at mine, frozen in fear. He must have felt just like an adult would feel who's had one too many drinks and hears the sirens of the highway patrol behind them. It's over, I'm caught. And there Brandon was at forty-two inches, standing under the line at forty-eight inches, a full six inches unaccounted for. The lifeguard continued, "I'm sorry, buddy." I started to plead with him. "Please, he can totally swim. I can go down before him so I can catch him when he comes down so you don't have to worry about him drowning, not that he would." The lifeguard continued, "If you want to have him professionally measured, you can do that in the office by the snack shack downstairs, ma'am."

Brandon just found out he wasn't tall enough to go on the roller coaster with Mackenzie and me.

I said, "Come on, Brandon, let's go in the lazy river instead."

"What, are you serious?" Brandon asked. "This isn't even a big slide. I've been on slides totally bigger than this dinky slide. Remember when you took me on the Hard Rock Hotel slide in Las Vegas, Mom? This can't be happening right now! This can't be happening right now!" He cried as he held his head in his hands in disbelief. I talked him down and said how it could have been worse by explaining what a DUI feels like, but halfway through I decided to offer him an ice-cream sandwich in exchange for him stopping his wailing and resigning himself to an afternoon in an inner tube.

As we finally entered Wild World, I said, "Brandon, now, some of the rides you are not going to be able to go on because you are not tall enough right now. One day you will be, but not now, and if you cry we'll have to go home. Do you understand?"

"Yes," he said. Or, lied.

I looked at the map and saw that the Lickety Split was forty-two inches, so Brandon made the cut to go on that one. After walking what felt like half a mile, we saw that the Lickety Split was closed. In fact, so many rides and restaurants were not open for business that Wild World was starting to feel like a foreclosure ghost town. Finally, we found the Wet 'n' Wonderful: it was open, Brandon was tall enough, and lo and behold the Express Pass worked on it. We got in a separate line and basically cut in front of the other people—my childhood dream was finally coming true! However, since it was December and not particularly hot outside, the ride was practically empty anyway. So it was 1:40 p.m. and we were finally on our first ride, which really didn't require the fifty-five-dollar Express Pass. Brandon liked it so much we went a few more times until we were totally soaked. I decided to buy the photo of us coming down the giant drop with all of our mouths agape. I went to the person in the booth and asked, "Can I get photo number 2423, sir?" When he turned fully around, I realized he wasn't a sir but a ma'am, and a ma'am who shaved. Her face had a complete five o'clock shadow, and it wasn't even two p.m. yet. That's always a scary thing.

One of the first articles I ever read in *Cosmopolitan* magazine when I was about eleven years old was about a woman who had to set her alarm clock and wake an hour before her husband did every morning so she could shave her face without her husband ever knowing her hairy secret. They had been married for eight years and she had never slept in. I saw on a documentary that it is supposed to be a status symbol if a woman can grow a beard or goatee in prison. Now, if I were in prison, I'd certainly be impressed, but the fact was, I was not incarcerated; I was at a supposedly family-friendly amusement park looking to capture memories. I thought about how if this had been eighty years ago, instead of working the photo booth at the Wet 'n' Wonderful she would have been a main attraction in the traveling carnival as the Bearded Lady, the star of the whole show. Talk about being born in the wrong era. After I paid seventeen dollars for the five-by-seven photo and my credit card was run, she informed me the machine was broken and I had to go to another booth to pick it up. She got out the map of the park and circled where I was to go. It appeared to be near the entrance, and since the kids were whining for food, I decided I'd pick it up on our way out.

When we got to the food area, it was packed and the lines were longer than at the most popular ride. We tried to find a restaurant to eat at, but they were all closed. The choice was burgers or pizza, so I chose the pizza line but after twenty minutes the line had not moved at all. Unfortunately, my fancy Express Pass did not work for the food line. I had reached the point where I felt the need to talk to strangers since we are all in the same boat like they were on the *Titanic*. "This is ridiculous," I said. "They can't close all but two food stands and not allow us to bring in any of our own food. I'm sorry that they are financially hurting, but aren't we all hurting in this recession? My stomach is hurting because they wouldn't let me bring in some granola bars. They could have at least disclosed the rides and restaurants that were closed on their website so we could have stuffed our faces before entering the park, right?" But no one in line responded. They just continued to stand there looking straight ahead, so I kept at it: "It's two o'clock and we've only been on one ride. My hamstrings are killing me from walking. I'm never coming here again. My kids are starving. I'm going to tweet about this." Finally a dad with a teenage daughter responded to my rant and said, "The pizza sucks. It's like biting into a pizza box. You should go to the burger line, it goes a lot quicker."

It wasn't until I was in the equally slow-moving burger line that I realized the guy just wanted to get rid of me. This is why America is where it is today—people just won't speak up at places like Wild World.

After my kids devoured their eleven-dollar burgers, we were off to ride the Flash, which is like a roller coaster that you hang from. Because Brandon was tall enough to ride it, we were able to use the Express Pass. There were two lines. The one to the right said EXPRESS PASS and the one to the left said ENTER HERE. 45 MINUTE WAIT. The Express Pass led us on the other side of the ride and we only had to wait a few minutes. I have to admit, looking at the commoners standing across from the ride made me feel a little superior, but also a little guilty, like Emma Stone's character in *The Help*. When the ride returned and the passengers were released, the people on the other side who were anxiously waiting started to move an inch forward when the conductor of the ride held up his hand to stop them and then ushered us, the VIPs, in. We could choose any seat we wanted, so of course I went for the front. Who wouldn't? As I hopped in and pulled down the bar around my shoulders and waist. I heard someone on my left, where the regular line was, say, "Really, lady, you're going to take the front row?" I felt bad because the people waiting to be in the first row had to wait even longer than the other people, but I didn't feel bad for too long because within seconds I was off jetting through trees like a flash. Brandon and Mackenzie were behind me. Drake was next to me and we were both screaming our lungs out the whole time.

About a half hour later, we were in line for the Monster, the largest roller coaster, when I checked my Twitter mentions and saw "Look who cut in front of the line at the Flash? It's the ugly girl from *Chelsea Lately*." And right there posted was the most unflattering picture of me getting into my seat.

It was a full close-up of my face, and I looked like I had two buckteeth and a double chin. The only view of myself that is more unflattering is when my iPhone camera accidentally reverses and faces me. Oh great, I thought, now I'm going to lose followers who are big amusement-park aficionados. And then I had an Oprah aha moment. I remembered when I used to come to Wild World with my parents and I would fantasize about one day being wealthy enough to rent out the entire park for a day so I'd never have to wait in line. Express Passes didn't exist back then, but essentially I was rich enough not to wait in line. I could afford to do something I had always dreamed of. I was so proud of myself. That is, until I overheard the two teenage employees talking to each other: "No way, man, I'm so tired. We were out at Skull's place drinking

Enjoying the roller coaster with Drake and Brandon.

till four a.m., then my shift started here at eight. I'll smoke a bowl with you though." Just at that moment we started to move forward. Nice, so the idiot in charge of running the roller coaster was hungover and functioning on four hours of sleep. As we chugged up to the first huge hill on the Monster, I looked out at the all-wooden ride and was horrified to see how it had deteriorated. The white paint was severely chipped and large chunks of wood were missing out of the planks. It was clearly infested with termites. At least Brandon was too small to ride and was off getting ice cream with my mother-in-law. Someone would survive to keep the family going.

After the ride did not kill any of us, but did give me some serious whiplash, we headed to the ice-cream shop. Brandon came running toward me crying and angrily screamed, "You went on a ride without me. What the heck is wrong with you? You're not my friend anymore!"

So for the next hour we used our Express Pass and rode Brandon's favorite ride, the Flash, over and over again, each time pissing off a whole new group of potential *Chelsea Lately* viewers. When we rode it for the last time, Brandon was on such a high he smacked a blond teenage girl's butt as he ran past her, saying, "Yeah, baby." I immediately went over to the girl and apologized. I couldn't believe it. The only explanation is that the caliber of gang members Brandon had been surrounded by all day had rubbed off on him. He was behaving like a little chauvinistic cholo.

That night when we were driving home, the kids were all saying what a fun day it was and that Wild World was the best place ever. I reminded them about the dirty bathrooms, about how upset I was when Drake accidently dropped his thirteen-dollar plastic cup (which provides free soda refills) off a ramp down a ditch, and how they only played Spanish music, but they kept saying that it was the best day ever. I relented and told them we could come back but we were not going to purchase the Express Pass. Drake piped up and said, "Did you not see the sign? It was a forty-five-minute wait for the Flash. That is like five hours in kid time. No way, Mom, we have to get the Express Pass every time."

I was worried that Drake was turning into one of those kids who have only flown privately and then when they board a commercial plane for the first time they shout to their parents, "Why are all these weird people on our plane?" But I thought about what a great time I had, despite riding the rickety Monster and Flash eight times, and said, "OK, but we're only going once a year." The next trip is on my calendar in solid red ink.

11

THE CHELSEA CLIQUE

Working at *Chelsea Lately* has many benefits, including free food, cooked by Chelsea's chef brother, Roy; health insurance; a 401(k) plan; and one benefit just for me: Chelsea especially likes to take me into her office to shave my face of its little baby hairs. Sometimes she'll just scream out, "Heather, come here! With this light, your hairy face will be so easy to get at." There are other female staff members with hairier faces than mine, but she doesn't feel comfortable asking them to be shaved.

All the writers vie for Miss Handler's attention. Like Chuy, we'd all like to be adopted by Miss Millionaire. But second to that, I enjoy all the opportunities to travel with her. And not just because it means getting to stay in hotels where I don't have to be a mom for five minutes. It is a wonderful bonding experience to go with Chelsea as her opening act for her live

The best Chelsea party ever: *Facts of Life* reunion sketch. I'm playing Blair's cousin Geri (who was a stand-up comic with cerebral palsy). Chelsea is Blair, Jen Kirkman is Jo, Loni Love is Tootie, Guy Branum is Natalie, and Brad Wollack is Mrs. Garrett.

stand-up shows around the country. But one thing she hates and does not allow is anyone crapping in the crapper of her private plane. It's a policy that, if broken, I believed could deeply doom someone and probably get mentioned in seven or eight *Chelsea Lately* round-table discussions.

One night Chelsea and I were traveling to Boston. She was asleep on the couch area of the chartered seven-seater plane. I had to go to the bathroom with the intention of peeing, but to my surprise a chocolate kiss of a poo came out. As I stared at it, I decided it was so little that it was really hardly noticeable. (I might add here that on these small planes the toilets just don't flush that well, and my little floater was there to stay.) I walked back and sat down to read more about Mackenzie Phillips having a consensual ten-year fucking relationship with her father. An hour later, Chelsea woke up and went to the bathroom. Within a minute she kicked open the bathroom door with her Louboutins and said, "Who the fuck left that little nugget of a shit in the toilet?" Her brother, Roy, and her assistant, Eva, both turned to me and in unison said, "Heather's the only one who has used the bathroom." I felt like a deer caught in the headlights. I manned-up to Chelsea and said, "Yes, I did do it. It was a little slippery sucker. I didn't intend for it to come out, but it did, Chelsea, it just did." She said to me, "You're disgusting," put her nightshades on, and went back to sleep.

The next week I don't think there was a day when she didn't bring it up on the round table. She beats a poop like a dead horse.

Almost a month later we were flying from New York to L.A. early in the morning. I enjoyed the fruit platter, coffee, and several delicious bran muffins. Really, Chelsea was asking for it. She could have just served us water. Anyway, I had to go pee again. And to my utter surprise, I simply let a morning shit go. As I heard it plop into the water, I realized its size and density. I thought, What the fuck do I do? Do I wrap it like a Tampax and put it in my purse? Or do I just resign from *Chelsea Lately,* go on unemployment, and tell my kids they have to go to public school? So I decided the less disgusting thing to do was to put a bunch of toilet paper down and around my belonging and try to cover it as best I could. It was kind of like being in a sequel to *Mission Impossible: Poo.*

I sprayed the perfumed Lysol that was in the bathroom until I felt nauseated from the fumes, composed myself, and left the bathroom. Everyone was sleeping due to a late night out after performing, so I tiptoed back to my seat to read my book about Carol Brady getting crabs from a onetime mayor of New York. The first person to wake up was Chelsea's Pilates instructor Tina, aka Tina Pilates. To keep her from going to the bathroom, I warned her that I wasn't feeling well and I had thrown up in there. Shortly after that, one of the two pilots went in and stayed for a while. Thank God, I thought, I can put the blame on him. If he loses his job over a poo for the rest of the Live Nation tour, well, so be it. My children were going to remain in private school.

I watched Chelsea sleep like a child I had just given birth to. I wanted her to stay asleep as long as possible, or at least until we reached Utah. Chelsea was half Mormon. Weren't they the forgiving types?

Chelsea in fact only woke up when we landed. I guess when she reads this she'll be in for quite the surprise. I laid a torpedo while she slept and I'm still working at *Chelsea Lately*—hopefully.

To this day, she still brings up the Hershey-size poo. Chelsea has a tendency to not let things die. A few years ago I was lucky enough to be one of the 140 people Chelsea chose to go to Cabo, Mexico, to celebrate her birthday. I brought Peter, whom I've never been able to figure out whether Chelsea likes or not. Still, he is my husband. On the last day I got drunk at the pool bar while standing in the pool. Local Mexican employees would come around and pour straight tequila down my throat. The only thing I love more than public displays of affection is PDA in a pool. As I got drunker, I had my legs wrapped around Peter and my tongue down his throat, making it hard for him to say, "Heather, stop it. This is a work party." I said with my hands in the air, "No, it's not! It's a vacation." He replied, "But you work with these people every day." And I said, "Just let me be me!"

Several staff members felt the need to take pictures of this moment, which maybe lasted much longer than a moment. We returned home the next day, and the following Monday night on the round table I was scared shitless that Chelsea would bring it up as a subject to be discussed. Luckily for me, she dedicated her entire opening monologue to my indiscretions. I would like to point out that I was making out with my husband of ten years. However, nobody brought up that Chris Franjola received a blowjob from a cougar stranger whom he proudly divulged treated him like a baby on a changing table. This all took place three hours into the trip and before the sun even went down—but no, I'm the drunken slut of the group. The photo of the tequila going down my face was featured at least ten times between the round table, opening monologue, and closing joke.

In March 2011, the *Chelsea Lately* show went to Sydney, Australia, for the second year. When we weren't filming shows, I had my heart set on a seaplane adventure. I had been hypnotized by them ever since *Fantasy Island*. I said to Chelsea, "If you book a seaplane, I know the seats are limited, but please let me come. I'll even pay my way. Then again, if you do something else, please invite me because I just want to hang out with you." She

said, "Yeah, yeah. We're going to do something fun tomorrow."
I went to sleep in my hotel dreaming of my upcoming fun day.
I woke up early and headed to breakfast, where I saw everyone. I was prepared for the day, with my backpack stuffed with
sunscreen, a towel, a change of clothes—everything. I wanted
to be prepared to go at a moment's notice. Chelsea was seated
with about six people, and I was ecstatic about the day ahead.
I put my backpack down on a seat next to them and said, "So
what are we all doing today?" to which they replied, "Oh, we
don't know. We're hungover." I said, "Well, even if you want to
just go to the beach, I'm game. I'm just going to go get some
breakfast from the buffet. I'll be right back." I was gone no
longer than four minutes (which is about how long it took the
chef to make my personalized omelet), but when I came back,
every single one of them was gone, even though their poached
eggs were still steaming. The only person left in the dining
room was Chuy. But when I sat next to him, he asked me to
get his breakfast because he couldn't reach the food. I said to
him, "Where did they all go?" To which he replied, "Oh, Miss
Heather, they went on a boating trip."

I was so upset. The year before when Chelsea took us on
a boat, it was a beautiful yacht with real crystal stemware
and the really good buttery Chardonnay, just the way I like
it. There were plenty of places to lie out and you could also
wear heels and feel comfortable walking around. That's the
kind of boat I prefer. So I was imagining them heading off
for a repeat of our last adventure, minus me, and I just didn't
know why. Chris Franjola, who now had joined us said,
"Heather, who gives a shit?" I said, "I give a shit, because I

asked to be included. Am I the nerd of the third grade who has lice? Because, Chris, I don't have lice. I mean, I know I have thick, luscious hair, but no one has ever nested in there before." Chuy said, "Oh, Miss Heather, I had lice in my eyebrow once, but that was back in prison."

I was hell-bent on the seaplane, and Chris suddenly said, "Chelsea sent me a text saying that a seaplane was available for us and to have fun." My dream had come true! I told Chuy and he said no, but then I said it was free and he said OK. This was perfect. I now had my own Tattoo from *Fantasy Island,* who I could make say, "Da plane, da plane."

I was still kind of pissed about the blow-off and it got in the way of my perfect seaplane experience. It took Chuy's philosophy about how beautiful life is for me to calm down and have fun. The plane dropped us off at a beach and that is where I made everyone pretend we were stranded like the cast of *Gilligan's Island.* I cast Fortune Feimster as the Skipper, Jiffy Wild as Gilligan, Chris Franjola as the Professor, Sarah Colonna as Mary Ann, and I, of course, was the movie star, Ginger. I didn't cast Chuy, because he was already a series regular on *Fantasy Island* playing Tattoo.

Later, Chuy gave me a massage. Feeling my muscles with his little nugget fingers is amazing because he can really get into the knots around my shoulder blades better than a masseuse with regular-size fingers. He said to me, "Oh, Miss Heather, you get too stressed out. You don't need Chelsea when you have me." Chuy really does have a decent heart. But a small part of me was still jealous.

When the seaplane came to pick us up and finish our tour,

I got to sit in the front next to the pilot, so I pretended I was a contestant on *The Bachelor* and the pilot was the Bachelor. But I guess something was lost in the American to Australian translation because when we landed he asked me out and I had to explain I was married and just improvising a reality show that had been on for nineteen seasons.

Chelsea and the others returned from their boating adventure and we all hooked up at dinner. It turns out the boat was a gift from the parents of one of Chelsea's friends, Amy (the stylist for the show) and it was Amy's choice as to who went along. It was like a little sailboat that you had to sail yourself and couldn't leave the Sydney marina. Apparently, Chelsea yelled at Josh Wolf (also a writer on *Chelsea Lately*) because he was supposed to be steering one of those sails where you had to watch your head or you would be decapitated. Even worse, there was no vodka on the boat. That three-hour ride for Chelsea made it the longest time she had ever been on a boat since she was ten without alcohol. I was beginning to see the merits of our adventure, felt bad for theirs, and kept telling them how wonderful the view was of Sydney that you could only see from a seaplane. Chelsea never gets jealous, but when I told her how Chuy and I reenacted the opening credits for *Fantasy Island,* I could see it was starting to affect her. She really should have been the one playing Mr. Roarke, since she had discovered Chuy after his porno days.

The week before the Super Bowl between the New York Giants and the New England Patriots in February 2012, there had been rumblings about who would be going to Chelsea's Super Bowl party. Slowly, one by one, I was hearing that all of the other writers were getting invites. Now, if there is one thing I like, it's a party with commoners and stars, and a halftime show starring Madonna. At Chelsea's, even if you have to take a bathroom break there's a television there too. It was a perfect Super Bowl Sunday, or so I thought it would be. Right before I was to go on the round table I saw Dan Maurio, a producer on the show, and I said, "Did you get invited to Chelsea's party?" And he said, "Yes, but only in passing." And I said, "Well, she's passed me seven times today and hasn't invited me. Does that mean something?" As we went to tape the round table, I finally just blurted it out on TV: "You know, Chelsea, I don't care about not being invited to your Super Bowl party. I'm going to have a great one with waterslides and a margarita machine, and my children, and even my husband, are welcome." She said, "I'm glad you have something to do in the Valley." I then said, "Well, I know sometimes I don't get invited because I'm a plus-four." She retorted, "Some people don't get invited if they're just one."

I ended up having a great time at my Super Bowl party, and when Madonna sang "Like a Prayer," my best friend Liz and I sang our hearts out, which would not have been well received at Chelsea's. Still, I felt a little hole in my heart when I saw paparazzi photos of Charlize Theron carrying a case of Dogfish Head Ale up the steep driveway toward Chelsea's house. This was my wasted chance to get into the *New York Post*'s "Page Six" column.

I later discovered that none of my colleagues even spoke

one word to Charlize. It's very possible that Chelsea thought that after a few Chardonnays I'd ask Charlize to re-create scenes with me from the movie *Monster,* which I knew by heart. In the movie she played the most notorious lesbian serial killer, and I was hoping to play her lesbian lover who testified against her. Admittedly, my asking Charlize to act out *Monster* was a sure thing. Of course, I don't know if Ms. Theron would have been up for it.

A couple weeks later, God intervened. Sarah Colonna pulled all of the writers into her office and shut the door. She said, "Chelsea wants to take all of us to Cabo this weekend. Who can go?" The first hand up was mine. There wouldn't even be guilt in my going, because I wasn't going to miss any family events, Little League baseball had ended, and Peter could watch the kids. My fellow writer Jen Kirkman said she couldn't go because her mother was in town. Chris and Brad had to work until midnight on Friday for Chelsea's NBC sitcom, where they punch up some of the lines. Sarah gathered the head count and took it to Chelsea. She returned ten minutes later and said, "Chelsea feels bad that Brad and Chris can't go because they're working on her show. Now she wants to go to Napa and leave on Saturday morning for wine tastings and a spa. Sarah asked again, "Who's in?" My hand went up immediately and I said, "Even better, a short flight away and wine." Thirty minutes later I strolled into Chelsea's office and said how excited I was. She looked at me and shook her head and said, "The forecast is rain. I really don't want to go wine tasting in a storm." I agreed.

She said, "Why don't we go out for a really great dinner on Saturday night with all of us." Oh great, I thought, I could buy a new dress and there would be paparazzi.

Friday afternoon, I got an e-mail from Chelsea's assistant saying dinner would now be at Chelsea's home. I thought, even better, she always has celebrities over, like Jen Aniston and Reese Witherspoon, who really enjoy a more intimate dinner party than being gawked at inside a crowded, noisy restaurant.

Saturday came around and it was rainy. That forced me to go from my new dress for the occasion to skinny jeans and my brand-new Jimmy Choo black knee-high boots, which really felt more Jennifer Aniston–esque than my first outfit. I even thought about spritzing on Jen's perfume but knew Chelsea would be horrified that I perfume-stalked her. When I got there, I parked down by the security gate and walked up the steep hill. I wanted to leave the spaces free by the front door for all of the celebrity drivers so they could have enough room to park and wait.

I rang the bell and no one answered. I thought, Oh, good, it's a loud party. This will be fun. The first person I saw was Roy, Chelsea's brother whom she lives with, wearing shorts and a dirty T-shirt, and he had bare feet. I saw that Chelsea was outside wearing essentially pajamas, sitting under her covered patio as the rain came down. I went outside and she introduced me to Gary, her new puppy. There was also her dog Chunk; her other dog Jax, a boxer; and her friend Hannah, who'd brought her dog. They all came over to greet me, smelling like dogs do when they're wet but multiplied by four. Chelsea said, "Oh, go grab some dinner. It's in the cartons from P.F. Chang's." So I went to her kitchen and around to her island, where all the containers were opened up. When I touched one it felt lukewarm, so I asked Roy for a microwave-safe plate, and he just pointed to a cabinet. Then I asked for a fork and knife, and he pointed toward a drawer. I got a plate and asked Roy if I could have a glass of wine. He pointed in the direction of a walk-in pantry. I said to him, "Which one am I allowed to have? Some of these look pretty expensive." He replied, "Oh, Heather, you can figure it out." I picked out one that I recognized as being about fifteen dollars. Now, since Roy had left, at this point, I had to find the fucking wine opener. Soon I was seated at Chelsea's long table made from a piece of wood that came over from Venice. Venice, Italy, not Venice, California. It was just me.

Slowly some of the other writers arrived, having come from other events. This was their second or third party. They hadn't banked their entire evening on Chelsea's get-together as I had. I tried to talk to Chelsea, but really, you can only have a dog's wet nose in your crotch for so long without feeling like you're cheating on your husband. After about two hours, I decided I wanted to go home. I went to give Chelsea a hug good-bye and to thank her for being such a gracious host. The dogs came to lick my boots one final time. I asked for the security number to get out, but Chelsea, being Chelsea, gave me the wrong one. I found myself in the rain, on an extremely steep incline in my narrow heels, trying not to fall and punching in the wrong code repeatedly. Finally Jiffy Wild called to say they'd given me the wrong code. "It's actually 3401."

I got in my car, relieved to go home, but started to smell something pungent. I had stepped in fucking puppy poo, and since it was from a puppy it was more like diarrhea. I had to pull over to a gas station and wipe it off, but it was already on my gas pedals and my car rug.

The next day, Chelsea said to everyone that she had tears in her eyes from laughing so hard when she remembered how I'd sat all by myself eating my heated-up P.F. Chang's. She later told me, "Wow, that was quite a change of a weekend for you. We went all the way from Cabo to Napa to a fancy restaurant to me in my pajamas at home; you must have been disappointed." Sure it was shitty, but that could all be wiped away when Peter took the car to get washed.

I hope I am invited again, because I think I displayed a lot of grace in the face of such adversity. And I honestly do think Chelsea's company is one of the best. Sometimes I wonder if the Hershey's Kiss I left on the plane left a lasting impression. I certainly hope not.

12

DEATH BECOMES HER

I am obsessed with the CBS News show *48 Hours Mystery,* which is sort of like *Dateline* but all of the stories involve infidelity, killing of a spouse, and disposing of dead bodies. I have to admit I am hypnotized by the stories that feature rich, attractive people. My favorite genre is murder while scuba diving. This always involves the rich husband, or boyfriend, killing his blond wife, or girlfriend. The typical story line goes as follows: the new bride is scared of the notion of scuba diving, but the loving new husband convinces her that it will help them bond as a couple, so she agrees.

Even though he's logged more than a thousand hours under the sea, on their first dive, they go down farther because he convinces her that there's much cooler fish lurking below. He then proceeds to lovingly hold her hand and lead her farther and farther into the abyss. In the next scene, he comes up to the boat alone.

He asks the rest of the divers, "Hey, has anyone seen my beautiful bride?" The Coast Guard comes, and days later they bring up her lifeless body. It is clear that someone had let all of the air out of her oxygen tank. The authorities become suspicious when they realize the husband had conveniently taken out a million-dollar insurance policy on the wife who only made $30,000 as a kindergarten teacher. On *Law & Order: SVU*, when Mariska Hargitay goes to question the husband, instead of being scared to death, like I would be, he walks around their home folding clothes, changing a lightbulb, and cooking a spaghetti dinner. Mariska, in her typical investigation, discovers that he had slept with the maid of honor at the couple's rehearsal dinner.

Peter is very comfortable around water. Whenever he attempts something dangerous, like tossing our two-year-old Drake into the pool at our friend's country club on Labor Day weekend, I don't object because every time I try he retorts, "Please, I was a lifeguard in San Diego." However, when Drake threw up French fries into the pool that weekend and the club had to close the pool for three hours because of Peter's lifeguard antics, I got annoyed. I'm sorry, but reminding people to reapply their sunscreen on the beach is a little different than being a member of SEAL Team Six.

However, Peter is himself an experienced scuba diver with many more hours underwater than me. A couple years into our marriage he told me he had business in Ecuador and we could go to the nearby Galápagos Islands for a few days to check out the reef there. I was excited for this vacation mostly because for once it would not include a timeshare presentation. Since our honeymoon, every trip we had taken involved hearing a ninety-minute speech on how we could be part owners of a world-class resort. Once the salesman had driven us around in a golf cart explaining how $350 a month was actually an investment in real estate, and we had to tell him no several times before he reluctantly gave us the $75 gift card to Cheesecake Factory that was included with our discounted room.

I was excited and I'm always up for the beach. All I heard was island, not fourth-grade field trip with animals like it turned out to be. We boarded a boat that was not the size of a Carnival Cruise, or even Beyoncé and Jay-Z's yacht. Instead, it looked like the boat from *Gilligan's Island*. This region of the Galápagos Islands is a protected habitat, and no fancy hotels can be built there, which is a real shame because hotels mean cocktails, and nature is much more enjoyable with a buzz on. Peter and I had bunk beds, so it wasn't even as romantic as I thought it would be. The second day, we were woken up at five a.m. to see turtles humping. I never knew how turtles did it, but they do it from behind, one on top of the other looking bored. Evolution is simply not that exciting.

After watching the turtle porn, I put on a cute sundress, with wedge heels and bangle bracelets that nearly doomed me when the sound of them clanging together apparently disturbed the blue-footed booby (the birds with the blue feet). Everybody else was wearing advanced Birkenstocks that can take you from water to sea to sand and the rocks. My wedge heels made my walking on the rocks more than wobbly. I wondered to myself, Why hadn't Peter told me more about this trip? I thought I'd be sipping Piña Coladas.

The next morning Peter said, "Boy, do I have a surprise for you! I paid extra so that we can go scuba diving today. The Galápagos is supposed to be better than the Great Barrier Reef."

I had by now acquired an entire hour and a half log time as a scuba diver. So I asked Peter how they were going to let me scuba dive if I wasn't properly certified. Peter then proudly displayed a PADI card with my name on it that he had illegally mocked up by scanning his real PADI certification card on the computer. I was flattered that he had taken the time to essentially make a fake ID for me. Peter and I then got onto a small boat with just a guide. We went out far, and way past the sand that felt like white flour on your feet. Peter said, "We're definitely going to see coral and big fish because nobody can kill them here."

As we did our daunting back flip into the ocean, we slowly went down into the super-clear water. Peter was right. I saw a giant lobster, big enough to feed a football team. Suddenly, I accidentally pushed the wrong button on my geared-up suit, and shot like a rocket all the way up to the clearing. I had no idea how to get back down, but what immediately disturbed me was that Peter didn't check on me. The guide came up and over to help me while Peter was busy counting colorful blow-fish. I had *48 Hours Mystery* running through my mind, and was just glad that I had made it out alive.

As much as I hate scuba diving, I am even more freaked out by skiing. When I was about six, I watched a made-for-TV movie about a girl named Sheila. She was on a professional college ski team and very competitive with her teammate Suzie. On the day of the big race, as she watched Suzie turn a particularly tricky corner, Sheila thought, "Suzie's going a little bit slow around that turn. Even though our coach warned us about going too fast around it, I bet I could cut a few seconds off and beat Suzie." Sheila swishes the snow off her highly waxed skis and when the buzzer sounds she takes the curve going faster than her coach told her to ever go. Immediately, she goes out of control and smashes through the mesh nets that line the side of the ski course. In the next scene, she's being raced through the hospital corridor with her eyes frantically moving from right to left, her head in a neck brace. Her family rushes in and says, "Will she ever ski again?" And the doctor says, "No, in fact, she'll never walk again." In the end, Suzie comes to Sheila's hospital room to bring her flowers and she's wearing a gold medal.

While my fear of skiing was deeply rooted thanks to Sheila, I did go to Lake Tahoe with my family at age nine, and was able to make my skis into the shape of a piece of pizza and French fries. However, I was never really interested in advancing further than that.

When I first started dating Peter, a skiing enthusiast, he took me on a trip to Mammoth Mountain in California. I told him to go ahead and go off on his own, as I took a lesson. We planned to meet for lunch (my favorite skiing activity) at noon, so by ten forty-five, I decided I didn't want to be late. Plus it takes a few minutes to take your skis off and place them against the wooden ski racks and then trudge through the snow into the warm lodge. By one, Peter was off again, which meant I had another four hours to kill. I told him I was taking another lesson, but instead I just had Bloody Marys and never went back outside.

Once we were married, the first six years we couldn't go skiing because we always had a newborn to take care of, and then they became toddlers, which are even worse. We started up again when Drake was a bit older, since we had a friend who had a four-bedroom house in Mammoth. A free vacation is a free vacation, even if it involves skiing and not a sunny beach. This time I was upfront with Peter and told him I really just wasn't into skiing. He was fine with my choice—he knew he hadn't married Suzy Chapstick. I told him he should also be grateful that I wouldn't need a knee replacement at fifty because I simply am not athletic. Plus, an added bonus to Peter, I was one less ski ticket to buy.

I did decide to put some of my fears aside on our next trip to Mammoth and agreed to ski with Brandon, then four, and Drake, who was seven. Drake could kind of snowplow, but I had to put Brandon on a reindeer's leash and take him down the slope, which really didn't slope too much at all. The lines were really slow and Brandon would start eating the dirty snow. After telling him three times to stop it, I just gave up.

Brandon right before he started to eat snow off the bottom of his ski.

The day just became more irritating as it went along. At one point, I was taking Brandon to the bathroom when a woman stopped me and said, "I know you probably hate this. But I just have to tell you I watch *Chelsea Lately* all of the time. And . . ." I had to cut her off because I could barely see Brandon's brown hair anymore in the crowd and I didn't want this to become an episode of *Without a Trace*. So I said to her, "I'm sorry but my son—" In a pissy tone of voice, she replied, "Oh, I know, I know. I'm sorry. I give you a half hour of my night five days a week and you can't spare one minute for me." She stormed off as I tried to speed walk in my ski boots, heel-toe, heel-toe, feeling like Jeremy Renner in the movie *The Hurt Locker,* breathing heavily in the bulky outfit he had to wear when he was attempting to detonate a bomb. I just hoped that some perverted man wouldn't offer to help Brandon out of his ski jumpsuit.

That night on Twitter, I received a tweet under mentions that said, "Saw @HeatherMcDonald skiing. What a bitch. Tried to tell her I liked the show. Guess she doesn't have time for fans." I don't know, sometimes you can't win. But on the cheery side, I had saved my son from sexual molestation.

We were staying at Peter's friend Marvin's four-bedroom house. He was recently divorced, and had a twenty-three-year-old girlfriend, Mimi, who was studying for her LSATs. Dinner the first night was fun because we got a sitter and went out. I felt reinvigorated reliving my USC days by talking to Mimi.

The next morning Brandon crawled into our bed and said to me, "Mommy, will you play Monopoly with me?" My heart started to beat with the possibility of an out for skiing. So I said to him, "Well, you have to make a choice. You can either go outside in the subzero weather and ski, or you can lie in the big cozy warm bed with Mommy all day and play Monopoly." He said without flinching, "I want to play Monopoly." I felt like I had won a big lottery scratch-off ticket. Drake said he didn't want to go skiing either, and asked if he could be the dog on the board game. There we were, the three of us, in the house with Mimi.

There was only one living room with a TV and that's where Mimi insisted on placing all of her study guides. This was the same room where we intended to play Monopoly. The huffing and puffing from Mimi that went on whenever one of the boys scored some property and got excited became annoying. Why didn't she move to a bedroom, or better yet the Starbucks right up the street? I tried to empathize, but it's been a long time since I studied for a test. It was a battle of wills. And I said to her, "I'm sorry. I know that when my sister studied for the LSATs seventeen years ago, she was a real bitch too."

Mimi replied, "Well, maybe I wouldn't be so bitchy if you had a handle on your kids."

This got me feeling defensive. "Well, frankly, I'm surprised you're so critical of them seeing as you're closer to their age than Marvin's."

She was seething. "Well, when Marvin and I have children, they certainly won't act like your monkeys."

I just blurted out "You bitch" at her, and she just said it right back. I said, "Really, as an aspiring attorney, that's your best counterargument? I hate to break it to you, but you're no Star Jones. I can't see you as a trial lawyer with your type of lame defenses."

Suddenly Mimi started to cry. I had obviously touched a raw nerve and this made me feel bad. I looked at the clock and it was already one, which is the time I normally start my après ski drinking anyway. I grabbed a bottle of wine and asked her if she would like a glass too. I turned on Nickelodeon—I knew the boys would stay glued to the TV so I could give Mimi some life advice.

I told it to her straight. "You're gorgeous. You're a size two on the most bloated day of your period, and you're smart, because you're going to law school. Do you really want to spend your precious twenties, while you're juggling torts and contracts, hanging out with a man in his mid-forties and his friends and their annoying families?"

I had Mimi's attention, so I continued, "Look, it's hot and sexy now to have a forty-three-year-old guy who wants to pork you in the office supply room." By the way, I'm a huge fan of illicit office sex, at least in movies. That is where the girl is wearing the tight pencil skirt and whoever the boss is just turns her around, pulls up the skirt around her waist, and does her right there next to the Xerox machine. I continued, "But, Mimi, then what happens? You get married and ten years later, sure, it's still kind of hot. He still likes to fuck and party. But twenty years later, and he's sixty-three and you're still a hot forty-three? He doesn't want to go out anymore. In fact, he's retired. And the Porsche hasn't been driven in six years. The sex swing? Well, that has a stack of folded laundry on it that his lazy wrinkled ass won't even put away for you.

You'll start hiding his Viagra and putting Xanax in his red wine so that he'll pass out and won't bother you. Mimi—that will be your reality."

Within an hour, I had talked Mimi out of her relationship. She was on her way to the Mammoth airport for a flight back to L.A.

I had some explaining to do to Marvin when he came home from the slopes. Not only was his house a mess, wine bottles emptied, and Monopoly money strewn throughout all four bedrooms, but his hot twenty-three-year-old girl-friend was gone too.

Needless to say, Peter lost a friend and we never got to stay at Marvin's plush ski house again.

This past year, we could afford not to bunk with anyone and stayed at the Westin at the foot of the mountain. Brandon took lessons from a Swiss ski instructor, who wouldn't take any of his five-year-old bullshit. Now he can ski, along with his brother and me. It was actually really fun. I'm going to start my own "It Gets Better" campaign just like gay celebrities have done in personal videos for gay teens telling them how it gets better in time. I'm going to get the word out to moms of very young children that when it comes to skiing, it gets better too (sorry, Marvin).

13

NOT WITH MY MAN YOU DON'T

In Woodland Hills, where I live, there are several mom groups and Internet listservs. A service matches you up with mothers of similar-aged children and you meet at a different mother's house each week, or perhaps even at a park. I was in a group with Elaine and her four-year-old son. We became insta-friends because, well to be honest, I wanted to list her house. Still she was fun and helped make the hour before naptime go by quicker. One evening we were on the phone and she screamed, "Goddammit, Bobby, you're such a fucking asshole. Every day, every fucking day, twenty-four hours a day it's all about fucking Bobby. Can't you just give me a minute so that I can talk on the phone with my friend Heather?" I was a little startled by the way she was talking to her husband and wanted to immediately get off the phone. I said, "Oh, your husband is home? Why don't you deal with him and then call me later?" She replied matter-of-factly, "Oh that's not my husband, that's Bobby Jr. Wait, hold on. 'I said get your own fucking Lucky Charms!'"

She had always said how happy she was that she gave up her job at CBS to raise her son, so this came as a shock to me. The following Thursday, the group met at an indoor play space called Jump & Fun. Bobby Jr. was playing with a boy named Kirby. They were immersed in the world of Thomas the train and his track. Kirby took Bobby Jr.'s train and cut in front of him on the track. When Elaine saw that, she started screaming at the child. "What do you think you're doing? My son, Bobby, was playing with that train." Just then the other boy's mother stepped in and said, "Whoa! I think we should let the boys work it out." Elaine said, "No, I'm not going to let it just rest. Your son is clearly a bully. I suggest you reprimand him now or I will consider filing assault charges against your four-year-old!" The other woman told Elaine she was being ridiculous and if she didn't stop, she would tell the owners of the play space. Elaine then made her way over to me and said in a huff, "Jesus, Mary, and Joseph, can you believe that fucker? Besides, she's too fat to even break it up. That's why she doesn't want to get involved." I said to Elaine, "Um, I do believe she mentioned she was seven months pregnant. I don't think you should be calling her a fat-ass."

Elaine felt like suddenly I was playing sides and I could tell some expletives were coming my way. "Fuck that, Heather, you seem very lax about everything, and I just don't think we share the same parenting philosophy. I don't think you have my or little Bobby's back." To which I said, "It's Thomas the train that we're talking about."

"No, Heather, it's more than just that. It's not over just a train. We've been growing apart for a long time now. I think it's time Bobby and I find another playground, so fuck you again. Bobby, come to Mommy, we're getting the fuck out of here."

It was good that she had decided to leave, because Jump & Fun's bouncer was about to escort her out anyway. I sure was going to miss Elaine's house parties. The last one had been for her husband's fortieth and she had roped off a VIP area, where she served more expensive wine. I was lucky enough to make the VIP list. Sure it felt awkward standing in the alcove area of her townhome, talking to someone in the living room area as I sipped my Cakebread Chardonnay while the non-VIPs drank their Trader Joe's Charles Shaw wine. We don't live in a communist society, and there are different classes of friends. Am I to feel guilty that I was placed in a higher caste?

Another woman who had witnessed Elaine's freak-out came over to me. "Hi, I'm Gigi. I was in a playgroup with Elaine a year ago, and she's insane. She accused my daughter of being a LEGO smuggler, and threatened to call the authorities on her."

Gigi and I hung out for the rest of the afternoon and formed our own alliance. She was the definition of a hot mom. She wasn't slutty in any way. She was just good-looking and had a really toned body. Her husband, Walter, was fun and friendly, so he and Peter became close. We started hanging out a lot.

During the summer they would come over often for our pool parties where we all got decked out in our swimsuits.

One day, we were having wine by the pool around two o'clock. I sensed some major tension between Walter and G, but I just placed it on the fact that it was the anniversary of 9/11 and he had a military background. They both disappeared into the house for a while and when I came in, G was just sitting at the kitchen table alone. I asked, "Where's Walter? Were you two getting it on in the laundry room? Ha-ha!"

She said, "No, he left."

I asked, "What? Why?"

To which she replied, "I don't know, Heather, he's just extremely jealous."

I asked, "Jealous of what?"

G said, "Walter thinks I go out to happy hour too often after work."

And I replied, "Well, G, maybe you should pare it down a little."

She interrupted me. "Heather, Peter would never tell you that you couldn't go to happy hour."

Actually, even if I wanted to go to happy hour, I couldn't. I work at *Chelsea Lately* until seven p.m. when the prices go back to full price. My happiest hour is when I get to go to bed at nine twenty p.m.

I felt a little bad for G and said, "Well, you know you can always talk to me about anything, even if you're having problems with Walter."

Within moments of my saying that, Walter leaped back through the front door, still in his swim trunks and barefoot.

He folded his arms and said, "Well, I'm glad G can talk to you, Heather, because she can't talk to me. Let me ask you, do you think it's appropriate that a married woman texts men at nine o'clock on a Sunday morning?"

G leapt up in her swimsuit and said, "Oh my God, Walter, you're so annoying. Can't you just leave me alone?" She quickly walked down the hall to get away from him. We both followed.

I was saying to them, "Wait a minute, you two. I think things are getting out of hand, and you don't mean what you're saying."

G said, "No, Walter, I just think you are so controlling all the time. I can't take it."

Walter turned to me and said, "How is it that a man caring about his wife and her well-being, and the character of people she associates with is considered controlling?"

All I wanted was for them to make up. I wasn't trained in marriage counseling, especially to couples in bathing suits, just real estate and comedy, so I said, "I don't want to see you two break up. You're not going to be able to sell your house for what you paid for it."

It had all escalated with trust issues, yet there was no evidence of anyone cheating. G started crying, so of course I did too, and then Peter opened the door suddenly in his bathing suit and said, "Hey, who's up for the hot tub?" He looked at the three of us, saw G and me crying, and uncomfortably said, "Well, I'll leave the heater and jets on for whenever you guys are ready." Then quickly shut the door.

A couple months later, Walter moved out and G became a single mom. Since I worked all day, she would call Peter to ask questions, like about how she could refinance her house. She continued on this track for months, but never once asked Peter to file the papers to get it going so that he would be her mortgage broker. Instead he was just giving her free advice.

Meanwhile, on weekends we still got together with G and her daughter, Emma. G said to me, "Oh, Emma said the cutest thing to me. She asked, When we get our new daddy, can he be just like Peter?"

I've never thought my husband would cheat, neither have I had any indication that he had or would, but it's still my biggest fear because I know that our marriage couldn't survive infidelity. We've all seen those women on *Oprah* who couldn't imagine that this would happen to them, so I forced myself to imagine what I would do if I discovered he was cheating. I would be incredibly friendly during the divorce. Everyone would say, "I can't believe how great you two are working this out." And I would reply, "Yes, we're doing it for the kids. And I actually do like Peter." But three years later, when everyone least suspected it, I would get my revenge. That's clearly the smartest way to murder your cheating spouse.

Of course, I've told this story to everyone I know, including Peter, so hopefully he won't cheat. Otherwise this book is some damning evidence for the prosecution.

I wasn't aware that I was the jealous type when I married Peter, but a year after our wedding we went on a vacation to Cancún. One night, I thought I was pretty groovy by saying, "Hey, darling. Let's go to a strip club." To which Peter said, "Well, how much will it cost?" And I said, "Peter, don't be frugal. We're on vacation and the strippers will be cheaper because we're in Mexico."

So we walked into Cancún's Gold Fingero Club and paid twenty dollars apiece to get in. At first we sat and watched a little of the show, where girls played on the stripper pole. I was impressed with their upper-arm strength and how they could flip themselves around like gymnasts at the Olympics. At this point they were sporting string bikinis and taking off their tops—full nips. I was totally fine with it. I was married, having sex regularly. I was very open to sexuality and none of it was bothering me. Admittedly, I was the coolest wife around.

We asked the proprietor for a lap dance, which would cost at least forty dollars, plus tip, depending on how much we enjoyed the experience. We were led into a little photo-booth type of room and Peter and I sat next to each other. Soon a cute little Mexican woman came in. She had an excellent body, nice, natural boobs, and pretty, brown long hair. She was wearing a bikini. So she turned on some music after drawing the curtain shut, and immediately started touching Peter and shoving her butt into his face. When I looked over at him, he was totally smiling. At first I thought, Oh good, he won't mind the money. But then out of the blue I turned into Glenn Close in *Fatal Attraction*. I put my arm in between them and said, "I don't like this one bit." The cute woman said, "Oh okaya, letta me giva you some atencióne!" She started to rub my boobs, and I started to cry. Peter immediately told her to stop. As we got up, he handed her a twenty-dollar bill (which impressed me). She said, "Wait, you paid for whole song. We're only halfway through." Peter said, "No, she can't handle it," and walked me out of Gold Fingero for a stroll along the beach.

Anyway, not since the strip club had I felt this kind of jealousy. So I said to Peter very firmly, "I don't want you talking to G anymore on the phone. She's never going to give you the loan. And I wouldn't want you to have her as a client anyway. If she calls again, tell her how busy you are and she should just go straight to her bank." He said OK, and I figured that was that.

Four days later, Peter called me at work and said he was at Chuck E. Cheese with the kids and that G had shown up. She apparently told him, "Oh, fancy meeting you here, Peter." He was frozen scared. He asked me if he was in the midst of a prank and if there were hidden cameras, because he certainly did not want to be on *Chelsea Lately* for this. He was convinced that Chelsea and I had set the whole thing up, but we hadn't. G and Peter just happened to go there at the same time.

Peter and I have always enjoyed role playing in our sex life. Well, I enjoy it more than he does because I'm an actor and he is not, so he has a little trouble getting into character and improvising a scene so that it reaches a climactic point, pun intended. He's a mortgage broker. I once came up with this one really good scenario, where I pretend to come to his office for a loan but I have really bad credit. I'm more than thirty days late on a Macy's credit card and I need to be punished *Fifty Shades of Grey* style. "Give it to me, Christian Grey." Then he has to teach me how to raise that FICO score to get the best rate. I like to play teenage hitchhiker or doctor, where he's the doctor and I don't have insurance but I need a breast exam and my yearly pap smear. My favorite is to play ABC's *The Bachelor,* where I pretend we are in the fantasy suite and I have to screw him better than the other two girls left in order to get the final rose and the Neil Lane engagement ring. Now, of course, we're very responsible during our sexy time and always make sure the children's Benadryl has set in. But this whole thing with G had got me thinking, so at my son's T-ball game, I said to Peter, "Let's pretend that we're both divorced and we're meeting at Little League for the first time." We made small talk. I asked him what he did for a living. And he bought me a Diet Coke at the snack shack. I got cold and he put his arm around me. I said, "My son and I are going for ice cream, would you care to join us after the game?" Peter said, "I'm sorry, I'm not interested in dating single mothers."

14

MY INAPPROPRIATE FRIEND

Lucy was a whole new kind of crazy. She was my good friend up until eighth grade, when she moved away to Orange County. Originally we pen-palled for about a year, but then that got tiring and I soon found myself writing letters that I forgot to mail. When MySpace came around years later, she wrote me and we reconnected. She lived only fifteen minutes away in the Valley. Lucy had a husband, Carl, a twelve-year-old daughter, and a three-year-old son.

We would watch episodes of *The Bachelor* together on the phone and dissect Bob Guiney (of season four) who was fat and thought of himself as hilarious. He sang all of the time and it was clear to us that he wanted to get a record deal and not a wife. He made out with girls left and right because he had that ugly-guy confidence that made no sense to either of us. I think the only bachelor who has surpassed Bob in his unattractiveness would have to be last year's Ben Flajnik, who would be perfect for playing a Geico caveman. Anyways, after watching the season together every Monday night from nine p.m. to eleven, we were beginning to talk to and see more and more of each other. Bob Guiney at least gave us that.

Often we would meet up for a walk and I noticed something about Lucy. Whenever we passed men, she would push out her J.Lo ass, flip her hair from one side to the other, and then giggle hello, starting up a conversation with them as if I wasn't there. These conversations lasted up to fifteen minutes and made me feel what it must be like to be a patient dog. Walking got a bit boring for Lucy after a while and she wanted to turn it up a notch.

One day during the blazing-hot summer, she called me and told me to meet her at a track and gave me the location. I had on a loose tank top and elastic-waist running shorts. I arrived at what turned out to be an all-boys' school, but assumed Lucy chose it because it was summer and school was out of session. Lucy, always late, showed up sporting just a hot-pink Nike jog bra, full stomach with abs exposed, and low-cut booty shorts. She said to me, "Today we're going to run." Not one to readily exercise, I thought, looking at her body, that maybe I needed to step it up a notch. Lucy and I started jogging, and I began to feel like there were eyes on us. Was I being paranoid? I looked up and saw forty teenage boys looking out an open window at us and whistling. This would have been my dream when I was a junior-varsity cheerleader, because at fifteen I was flat as a board, and didn't have these boobs. I was a late bloomer.

I told Lucy we needed to stop. I simply was not comfortable with these teenage boys whacking off to us, especially because only the weird ones are required to be in summer school. Plus, I was a mother to two boys at the time, not to mention a wife.

"Fine," Lucy said, annoyed. "Let me go to the vending machine and get a bottle of water."

I stood off to the side, still feeling a bit naked in front of these boys, in deep fear they'd be let out for recess. At that point I would have felt safer playing basketball in the San Quentin prison yard with lifers.

When I looked over, I saw Lucy pouring water over her chest as if she was Daisy Duke from *The Dukes of Hazzard,* the version starring Jessica Simpson. At that point I headed to my car, turned back again, and saw her talking to a boy who was standing near the soda machine. I beeped, and after lingering for a bit with the boy, Lucy finally came over.

I said, "Lucy, how old was that boy? Who are you, Mary Kay Letourneau?"

She said, "What? I was just being friendly."

Aside from those walks with her flirting with men, I didn't know her chattiness extended to boys who were young enough to be her son.

We were now on to a new season of *The Bachelorette*, starring a Bob Guiney's reject. Once again we were engrossed in the multiple helicopter rides, fondling in hot tubs, and Chris Harrison's wise words. Our viewing was enhanced by gallons of wine. Laughing our way through a new episode, I said to Lucy, "Can you believe how quickly love can move along?" referring to the typical eight-week courtship. Lucy replied, giggling, "Heather, I have something I want to tell you. Jeremy now calls me every night. We have amazing chemistry and just this unexplainable connection. Just like they talk about it on *The Bachelor*."

I said, "Jeremy? Who the heck is Jeremy?"

Lucy continued. "Well, remember that day we were jogging at the track? I gave Jeremy my number and things just started to progress. I mean, love shouldn't have an age, should it?"

I was shocked. I said, "How old is Jeremy?"

She replied, "He's a senior. He's the quarterback and wanted to work out with me, so I said OK. He says I'm not like other girls."

To which I retorted, "It's because you're not a girl. You're a married mom."

"Oh, Heather," she said. "You're so judgmental."

I said, "No, Lucy, you'll be seeing a judge. . . ."

She interrupted, "It's not like I've gone all the way with him."

I said, "Why? Are you saving it for prom night, to make it extra-special? You really have to cut this out. I have moral issues with this whole thing."

We moved on, and I assumed she had stopped her involvement with Jeremy the jailbait. I think the biggest problem with Lucy was that she craved attention. That was becoming very obvious to me. For one thing, every time we went out to a restaurant for lunch, she'd tell the waiter it was her son's birthday and insist that the waiters gather at our table and sing to him. Then one day, when she called me on her Bluetooth while driving home from the mall with her thirteen-year-old daughter in the back, she said, "Heather, you're not going to believe it. Have you ever heard of the rapper Chocolate-C?"

I said, "No. And I like rap music."

Lucy then said, "Well, he approached me with his CD in front of Hot Dog on a Stick and said I had the most beautiful body he had ever seen. He asked me to be in one of his music videos, how about that?"

Her daughter, Casey, chimed in, "Mom, it was just to be an extra."

Lucy screamed, "It was to be a lead dancer, Casey, show some respect! He said I had a better ass than Beyoncé."

The way she spoke to her daughter and the competitiveness really bothered me. But I sympathized with her because she was having a lot of marital problems. Carl was kind of an odd dude, and we never really socialized with him. I always thought it might have to do with Lucy's proclivity to flirt.

One day I went over to her house in the Valley, with my son Drake, who was three at the time, to play with her three-year-old. As we were drinking coffee and eating some fresh strawberries, she said, "What are the days that you're most fertile in the month?" This woman had been having her period for more than twenty years. Shouldn't she know her cycle by now?

I said to her, "Well, it's fourteen days before you expect your period. Why are you asking me?"

"Well, you know that guy Roger from the gym?"

"No, I don't go to the gym," I replied.

"I saw him at happy hour last night. He has really cute dimples, so I went back to his place and you know. It just happened. Sorry, Heather, I'm not a nun."

I replied, "Wait, when do you get your period?"

Lucy looked at her calendar and said, "The twenty-eighth."

I said, "Today is the fifteenth, so that's a day over. You boned on the most fertile day of the month. I am guessing you didn't use a condom?"

"No, he didn't have one and neither did his roommate. Besides, I'm pretty sure I'm allergic to latex."

"Wait, he has a roommate? You're cheating with a man who can't even financially live on his own?" I asked in disbelief. "Forget that. Lucy, you have to get the morning-after pill right now."

"Oh, I don't know about that, Heather. I don't like to put anything unnatural into my body. My body is my temple and it's very sacred to me."

I was horrified and said, "Is sperm from a guy you met at the gym considered one hundred percent natural to you?"

"Well, I don't know if I mind having another baby. I mean, we should go to the gym just so you can see his dimples. Besides, he has dark hair like Carl."

I was perplexed. I said, "Would you really try and pass off another man's child to your husband and have him raise it as his own?"

"Carl never questioned me about him," Lucy replied, looking down at her son.

I knew I was done with her, but I felt this need to rectify the situation and I didn't trust she would get the pill. Back then you needed a prescription for it, so I called my gyno and got one. I went to the Target pharmacy to pick it up and, lo and behold, the woman in the red shirt behind the counter was the gossipy mother from my son Drake's preschool. Who knew that she could be into so many people's business and still hold down a job as a pharmacy assistant? As she rang me up, looking at the name of the prescription, she said, oozing with sarcasm, "Isn't this interesting!"

I retorted, "Well, it's not for me." And she grabbed the little white bag back and said, "If it's not for you, then legally I can't give it to you."

Pulling the little white bag back, I said, "Fine, it is for me. I just didn't want to admit it."

When I got to Lucy's house, I acted like I was in *Girl, Interrupted* and made her swallow the morning-after pill in front of me, checking under her tongue and the roof of her mouth to make sure it actually went down.

I went to get Drake, who was playing in what I thought was the playroom. The boys had gotten into some boxes and were now playing sword fights with dildos. My son was winning because he was holding a black one, and it was so much larger than Lucy's son's white one.

"What is going on in here!" I screamed to Lucy as I looked down to see more sex toys, lubricants, and DVDs that would make Jenna Jameson blush.

Lucy said, "What's the big deal? I'm just a small-time distributor of porn to help with the income. It's not like I'm in porn . . . anymore."

I was out of there as Drake was crying that he wanted his big black sword.

Note to self: defriend.

15

B-DAY PARTY

When I was in the second grade, I passed out eight birthday invitations to my eight favorite girlfriends in the classroom. On that same morning, one of my lucky invitees passed out invites to *her* birthday party, which was on the same day, at the same time. So guess who didn't get invited? Me. She didn't invite me! Had she not seen my Cindy Brady impression, where I lisp about my doll, Kitty Karry-All? It was hilarious. Worse, almost all of the girls she invited I had also invited to my party. One by one they came up to me to thank me for the invite but they just got Mary's and were going to attend her party instead. I guess because Mary was more popular and, to be honest, just more normal than me. Only my best friend, Liz, said she would come to my party. Even in the second grade, Liz had my back and said to me, "No matter who comes or doesn't come to your party, I will be there." That night the phone rang and I overheard my mother talking to Mary's mother. My mother said, "Why, of course we'll change our date to the following Saturday. That is no problem." Why the hell do we need to change our date? I thought. The next morning in class, Mary approached my desk with a small square envelope with my name on it and said, "Heather, I forgot this at home yesterday. It's your invite to my birthday party and I really want you to come." I had to fight back the tears, it was so sweet of her to say. It's the same emotional feeling I get when I imagine my eulogy and all my family and friends finally seeing what an incredible person I was. When I opened the invite it said, "Come to Mary's for a swimming sleepover." Shit, it was the exact same party I was planning to have. She even boasted she was going to have a Carvel ice-cream birthday cake like I was planning to have. Her party was the Saturday before the last few days of school, and mine was to be the night after the last day, which was a Thursday.

Finally, my big day arrived. The party was supposed to begin at noon, but by twelve thirty the only loser there besides me was Liz. My mom got out the school directory and started calling the other invitees' homes. Everyone had forgotten. Really, in one day since school was over everyone forgot? What bullshit. A few managed to come, but some were already gone for the day and cell phones didn't exist yet. In fact, even Mary didn't manage to make it. However, it turned out to be a pretty fun party and there was a lot more room to lay out our sleeping bags on our living-room floor than if everyone had showed up. The whole experience really affected me (hence me writing about it thirty years later). Mary went on to get married and divorced twice. I'm not saying that had anything to do with her not inviting me, forcing me to change my party to a week later, and then failing to show up. I'm just saying that is how her life turned out.

Liz at my birthday party. Even back then she had my back and loved hearing my stories.

So for my kids' birthdays, I want to make sure that (a) no one's feelings get hurt because they are not invited (the classes are too large to invite everyone) and (b) people remember to show up once they've RSVP'd. I explained to my children that we were mailing the invites to their friends' homes and that they are not to talk about the impending party at school, or about how fun it was on the school playground afterward. In other words, keep it on the DL (the down-low, but since they're children I've never explained that DL is also code for black men who fuck men on the side while being married to women).

As you probably know from watching *Chelsea Lately,* the staff is quite social. However, not everyone is invited to everything, and even worse, that not-invited someone is often me. The reasons behind it are the usual: "But you have kids, and you're married." Yeah, so what? I'll dump them for a fun Sunday brunch with Chelsea and friends with unlimited Bloody Marys. Just invite me. Let me decide if my spending time on a Sunday with my family is that important. I just hate it when on a Monday morning, while we're all gathering in the writers' room, I have to be subjected to the twenty minutes of conversation from my cowriters and supposed friends that goes something like this: "You should have seen Brad Friday night at Jen Aniston's house. He was so wasted he was just mumbling to her about how he cried when she and Ross finally got together. Oh, it was bad, and then on Saturday, we're in Chelsea's pool and Brad starts up again with the exact same boring story he told the night before while Jennifer is just trying to get a tan on the floatie. Like she wants to hear that?" And I'm thinking, Wait, they not only went to Jennifer Aniston's house on Friday but then hung out with her on Saturday too? I'm the one who does the Jen Aniston impression. I should have been invited to at least one of the events. Then from Steve Marmalstein: "I came later, just for dinner on Saturday night, but sure enough between the second and third course, there is Brad talking Jen's ear off again." Marmalstein was invited? He's not even a round-table regular, only on *After Lately.* I couldn't stand it any longer and I said, "Did any of you go to kindergarten? You are not supposed to talk about the party in front of people who were not included. Can you just keep it on the down-low like black men who are gay?" Then Jen Kirkman says, "No, Heather, we thought about calling you on Sunday when Chelsea texted us saying to meet her at the Hotel Bel-Air for brunch, but then we knew how you and your family go to church." There was a Sunday party too? We blow off church all the time, especially when it's brunch at the Bel-Air with Chelsea. "God, do you not know what happened to me in the second grade?" I cried.

"Yes, we do know, and that is one of the reasons we don't invite you. You repeat stories even more than Brad," said Chris.

We've been pretty lucky with the boys' parties. When they were little, we would rent out an indoor play place for two hours, but when my son Drake was turning eight I wanted to do something a little more special, so I booked a bowling party. Peter was bitching about it because Drake's birthday is October 29, so for the past four years we would have a combo birthday-Halloween party, and the activity was trick-or-treating and the gift bag was the candy they collected from the neighbors—easy and cheap. I put my foot down and just said, "Peter, don't worry about it. I'm doing everything. Just show up on Saturday at one p.m. at the Woodland Hills Bowl."

The Bowl is your typical slightly rundown bowling alley. It hasn't changed much since I went there as a kid. When I arrived with Drake, Brandon, and Mackenzie, I noticed several vans in the parking lot. I didn't think much of it and as we were walking into the establishment, we saw a group of handicapped and mentally challenged adults. My kids know how to act around people who are "special," so that didn't make me nervous, but when we got inside and noticed that every single lane except for two in the middle were being enjoyed by severely handicapped adults, I did get nervous. The hostess took us to the two reserved lanes for our party, which was smack in the middle of the Special Olympics. And then here comes Peter. This is what I hate. Whenever I seem to take charge of something that he is not behind, for example, this bowling party, it's a disaster and I hate that he gets to be right about yet another thing. I walked right up to Peter and said, "OK, I forgot that there is nothing that adults with Down Syndrome enjoy more than bowling, but I think this could be good for the kids to interact with them and therefore learn to be compassionate and grateful." Peter responded by saying, "Whatever you say. It was your idea, your party." As I helped my kids put on their bowling shoes before their guests arrived, one of the bowlers to our right came up to me and handed a disposable camera to her friend and then put her arm around me and said, "Take a picture, take a picture." I smiled for the picture as I always do. I have to admit I was a little surprised that they watched *Chelsea Lately,* but apparently we appeal to a very wide audience, and to be honest our jokes aren't the most sophisticated. Then she went up to Peter and did the same thing. "Take a picture, take a picture." So he took a picture with her. This woman wasn't a fan of mine, she was just a fan of taking pictures. Soon, she was in our lane and wanted to be part of our group. Drake knew not to say anything, so he whispered to me, "Mom, she's holding my ball." I thought this was strange even for her because every one of the special-needs bowlers had their own personalized balls with matching shoes and shirts based on their teams. I guess the same day as Drake's birthday was some kind of tournament for them. So I went over to her and said as nicely as I could, "I'm sorry, that is my son's ball and we only have enough room for his friends to play in this lane." She then angrily gave me the seven-pound ball back and said, "Chuy is funny. You're not funny!" and stormed off to her bowling team. She then pointed me out to her teammates who all started laughing at me. That is when I decided I'd had enough. No one tells me that I'm less funny than Chuy Bravo, especially on my son's eighth birthday. So I talked to our hostess and she was able to move us to the last two lanes of the bowling alley so we were somewhat off by ourselves. Drake ended up having a great day, and when we were leaving I saw the woman who'd criticized my comedic talent roll her bowling ball into the gutter and I felt a real sense of satisfaction.

This year, it was Brandon's sixth birthday on January 21, and being January it's too risky to plan anything outside, even in sunny Southern California. I was really busy at work, so I told Peter to plan the whole thing and then bugged the shit out of him, making him call and e-mail each parent who had RSVP'd two days before, and then the day before, to remind them about Brandon's party on Saturday. Again I didn't want just Liz and her son to be the only two to show up as a bitter reminder of my own childhood birthday disaster. Peter chose a new indoor play place called Jump & Fly. It had just opened up the month before and was a huge hit on the kid party circuit. It's a bunch of trampolines in several different areas in bright blue, yellow, and hot pink, so the place really feels alive. It is too large to rent out the entire place, but they offer party packages where you get a table and pizza, but you bring the cake. The only thing I had to do per Peter's instruction was to buy twenty stuffed Angry Birds. The Angry Birds were advertised as 70 percent off at Ralphs grocery store. When we found them in the bin at Ralphs, they were listed at $11.99. I got twenty, but then as I was about to check out I saw small Angry Birds that clip onto your backpack listed at $7.99 but were 70 percent off. Being married for eleven and half years at the time I was sure those were the ones Peter was referring to. So I took all the big ones out of my cart and bought the twenty small ones. When I got home, I proudly said, "I got all the Angry Birds for the gift bags for only $2.40 each." Peter looked in the bag and said, "Not those, the medium-size ones." This was one of the more surprising moments in my marriage. "But these are cheaper," I argued. "Yes, but for only about a buck more each kid goes home with one four times the size; that's a good party gift. Didn't you do the math?" I was dumbfounded. "The math? I thought if I came home with twenty large Angry Birds, you would have been angrier than all the birds combined and I wasn't interested in spending the night at a battered-women's shelter, so I switched them out for the less-expensive ones." (No, Peter's never hit me. Yes, I like to exaggerate for dramatic purposes.) The only time he ever went for a more expensive item was when it came to toilet paper. I guess now I know that when it comes to Angry Birds, or Peter's asshole, money is no object.

A half hour before we were to leave for Brandon's big party, I got a text from my sister Shannon, who was on her way, saying, "We got caught in a sandstorm, I couldn't see. We had to turn around, so sorry." A sandstorm? What the hell is that? Shannon had lived in the Palm Springs area for more than thirteen years and this had never happened. Was she in Dubai? I called bullshit and texted her, saying basically that. It pissed me off because she was three hours late for Christmas and I never said anything and she canceled the week before to meet us in Mammoth and I never said anything—so today I decided to say something. She wrote me back a pretty angry text, saying, "I'm sorry, you've never experienced a sandstorm but I'm still shaking from it. None of us wanted to miss Brandon's party." I knew she wouldn't want to miss it, but I was getting that panicked feeling. She has two kids, so that was now two fewer party guests, and two extra Angry Birds. I just wrote back, "OK" and yelled at my kids to get their shoes on.

Peter left with Drake to pick up Brandon's cake, and I was to meet him at Jump & Fly with Brandon and Mackenzie. Just as I was buckling myself into the car, my phone rings and it's Peter but all I hear is, "It's Brandon Dobias. Can you check again? It's his birthday." Oh my God, Jump & Fly lost his reservation was all I could think of. "Peter, Peter!" I yelled into the Bluetooth in my car. Then I realized he'd butt-dialed me, so I continued to listen. "Oh, the cake looks great, thanks," he said. I hung up and told myself to just relax, but how could I when we drove up to Jump & Fly and it was packed with minivans and huge Suburbans beeping and trying to fit into compact-car parking spots. Jump & Fly, with all the jumping on trampolines, provides a great workout, so every fat kid in the Valley was being dragged there by a parent. Also, it had rained that morning, so it was even more crowded due to soccer games being canceled. We finally got a spot. Too bad there were no designated parking places for parents spending hundreds of dollars on a party.

When we entered, a few parents I recognized from our school were already there and had a look of disbelief on their faces. The place was wild. It was like a kids' nightclub, and "I'm Sexy, and I Know It" was blaring through the loudspeakers. There were kids ranging in age from two to seventeen. One of the mothers from Brandon's kindergarten class held her daughter close to her thigh and said, "Wow, we've never been here. This is quite a place." "Yes, just think of it as New Year's Eve in Las Vegas," I joked. I went up to the front desk and screamed to be heard over the fist-pumping jams. "Hi, I'm Brandon Dobias's mom, Heather. Our party started at one thirty, but I just got here; there was no parking."

"Yes, I'm Kadisha. I'm your party host. I'm supposed to show you to your table, but I'm too busy to do that right now."

"So what do we do?" I asked.

"The kids can just jump on any trampoline and then we'll bring pizza to your table at two thirty," she said.

"Wait, that's it? How do we come together as a group?" I said as I turned around only to see the back of Brandon's shirt as he ran away from me and began hopping from one trampoline to the next.

I continued. "Is there anything we can do extra to bring

the group together besides eating pizza? This place is enormous."

"Well, you can reserve the dodgeball VIP trampoline room for a half hour, but it's an extra fifty dollars," she suggested.

Ugh. Cheap Peter, he'll pay for larger Angry Birds but not the one thing that would make the party decent. "Yes, we'll do it," I said.

"OK, from two to two thirty it will be yours," she said.

"Well, can you announce it so everyone knows?" I asked, and she said she would.

Mackenzie had invited a friend so she'd have someone to hang out with, but the girl's mother had dropped her off without signing the consent form. For a second I thought I'd just sign one and say she was my daughter too but then I saw a teenage boy attempt to do a backflip and land on his nose, which was now bleeding profusely, so I decided that would not be a good idea. I said to Mackenzie's friend, "Honey, call your mom to come back. She has to sign it." Just then an announcement came on, stating it was time for cake for an inaudible name. You couldn't understand it over the techno portions of Rihanna's "We Found Love", so I set out to find every parent who looked remotely familiar from the school parking lot to tell them to go to the VIP trampoline at two o'clock. As I approached one mother, she said, "You know they have a big sign at Brandon's birthday table that reads HAPPY 4TH BIRTHDAY BRANDON?" No, I didn't know that because Kadisha never showed me to our table. I mean, could anything be more traumatic to a six-year-old boy on his birthday than having a big sign say "Happy 4th Birthday"? This had to be fixed ASAP before Brandon saw it, or he'd lose his shit. In his mind, a four-year-old is a baby, and he's no fucking baby.

I ran immediately over to Kadisha and told her about the sign and she assured me it would be changed. Then I continued to remind everyone about our VIP party, which was happening in minutes.

At two, I start ushering in the kids and their parents like a bouncer at a club on Sunset Boulevard until I believed everyone was in. I noticed one boy who did not look familiar at all and seemed much too old to be in Brandon's class. I went up to him and said, "I'm sorry, honey, this is a private party."

Then Peter came up to me and said, "No, that's Carter, he's Brandon's best friend."

That always makes a working mother feel great—when she doesn't recognize her son's best friend. "Are you sure? He's huge!" I asked. Peter said, "His parents held him back a couple of grades so that he would excel at sports." It seemed to be paying off. No kid was safe. Carter was knocking children half his size down with the ball. One of those kids was Brandon, who I could tell was getting frustrated, because every time he tried to grab a ball, someone else got to it first. The fourth time it happened, he crunched down and started to fake cry. Goddammit, I thought. This party is costing me roughly seven hundred dollars. My son is not going to cry. So I went over to him and said, "Brandon, everybody can have the ball if they get to it first. That's how the game works. Now, you better start having fun and stop crying or I'm going to give all your birthday presents away to poor kids." Brandon looked at me for a moment and then said, "As if you know any poor kids. I'm sexy and I know it." And he wiggled his hips to the song, which was now playing for the fourth time, and hopped away.

I first realized Brandon was on to my threats about "poor kids" after we'd had an incident at Bank of America. My boys occasionally watched *The Amazing Race* with my husband and me, and every time they watched, no matter the season, it seemed like the contestants were in India. Drake and Brandon were shocked by the poverty. I'd say, "Yes, that is how lucky you are, see?" For the next couple of months, every time one of them wouldn't do what I'd ask, like brush their teeth or pick up their room, I'd say, "I'm sending you to India and I'm going to trade you for a nice Indian boy who will be so grateful just to have a toilet in his home that he'll do anything I ask."

Sometimes when the boys would complain about the tomato sauce being too chunky in the spaghetti I would say, "Oh, I e-mailed Rashid's mother in India and she said he loves chunky spaghetti sauce and can't wait to come here and live in your room. She said she's very excited to have you boys. Apparently they have a lovely hut and some new sticks and rocks to play with." Maybe it wasn't the most conventional way of parenting, but it was something fun we did at home as a family. It continued and it became a joke between the two of them. So when Brandon would disobey me, Drake would chime in and say, "You're going to India" and taunt him, and Brandon would do the same to Drake. So, one day I had to go inside the bank, which nowadays is very rare. I had the two boys and I sat them in two chairs at a loan officer's desk who was out for lunch and I started doing my business with the teller. I could hear them talking and getting rambunctious but didn't bother to reprimand them because I was almost finished with my transaction. When I heard Drake say to Brandon, "You're bad. You're going to India," Brandon got so upset, he hit Drake and yelled back, "No, *you're* bad! Mom is going to send *you* to India." Drake fought back, saying, "You're the one who just hit me. Na-na-na-na, you're going to India! You're going to have to poo in the streets with the cows." I tried to hurry up because I could feel it escalating as I was putting my checkbook back into my purse. Then I heard Brandon yell, "No, you're going to India and the cows in the street are going to eat while you wipe your butt with your hand after everyone in the town sees you pooing." Brandon was so mad at Drake because Drake kept laughing as Brandon was hitting him. Drake kept on: "You're going to be sent to disgusting India to live forever and your only toys will be flies!" Just as I was about to turn around and scold them, I looked up and realized that not only was my teller Indian but the other four people working behind the glass were Indian too, and the customer to my right was an older woman in full Sari dress with a ruby dot on her forehead. So I did what I believe any mother in my situation would do. I looked at my teller's big dark kohl-eyeliner eyes and said, "Whose kids are those? Why don't people learn to watch their children? Thank you so much." Then I began speed-walking out of the bank. Just as my hand touched the door to escape, I heard the familiar sound of footsteps running after me, and Drake and Brandon yelling, "Wait, Mom, don't leave without us!" Thank Vishnu for online banking, because I haven't had to return to the bank since.

Anyway, halfway through our VIP half hour at Jump & Fly, Brandon grabbed my hand and said, "Jump with me, Mom." I was in the middle of a juicy conversation with one of the mothers about how she believed another mother in their Girl Scout troop was guilty of extortion. Extorting what, I wondered. Thin Mints cookies? It certainly wasn't going to be the Samoas cookies with the coconut. No one would risk anything for those. But then I thought, Next year Brandon may not ask me to join him at his party, so I started to jump. And the moment my feet landed, I felt a trickle of pee drop into my underwear and then more, and then more. I started laughing so much at the fact that I couldn't control the pee, even more came out. Ladies, if you've given birth, especially more than once, do not attempt jumping on a trampoline without a panty liner. No, I take that back. Make it a thick pad with wings. Liz then interrupted my jumping and my peeing to tell me that Brandon's birthday table still read "Happy Fourth Birthday" and we were five minutes from the pizza being served.

I immediately ran over to Kadisha, crossed my legs to keep any more pee from coming out, and said, "Someone needs to change my son's birthday sign from fourth to sixth birthday before he sees it. It's 2:26 p.m. Pizza is at 2:30. It's time, it's time." I felt like Academy Award–winner Shirley MacLaine in *Terms of Endearment* when she freaks out at the nurses because it's time for her daughter, played by Debra Winger, to get her pain pill. Finally Kadisha put a little spring in her step and said, "I've got it right here, I'll run up there now, ma'am."

"Thank you," I said, and just like Shirley did in the movie,

I pushed my hair from my face, straightened my blouse, and ran to the bathroom.

After the pizza was devoured, I realized there was about to be a severe water shortage at our table. Water is by far the most coveted natural resource at Jump & Fly. All the kids have bright-red cheeks with sweat pouring down their foreheads and are huffing and puffing and begging for water. There are no water fountains, only vending machines with bottled water at two dollars a pop. As part of our package we got twenty small bottles of water but we went through those quite quickly. "Kadisha, we need more waters, please," I requested.

"It's going to cost you extra," she said.

"Not as much as it is going to cost me if one of these kids passes out from dehydration. Get the water, I don't care what it costs." Then I turned to Peter and said, "You picked this place, so you're not allowed to bitch about the price. The kids need to have water. At least we have the option to buy clean bottled water, unlike the people in India." The way the kids were grabbing at the bottles I felt as if I were a combat Marine passing out water in an Iraqi orphanage.

That night, after Brandon opened his gifts and I was having a glass of wine, I turned on the TV and the top story of the evening news was "Sandstorms Hit Palm Springs."

16

THREE WEDDINGS AND NO FUNERAL

I first met Joe Francis, creator of the Girls Gone Wild franchise, when he was a guest on *Chelsea Lately* in our first season. We hung out a few times at events and he just took to Peter and me. Once, he even asked Peter to join him for a guys weekend at his mansion in Mexico. I put my foot down on that one. A guys weekend with Joe Francis would be second only to one with Hugh Hefner (Hugh would probably fall asleep and Peter would have the only working penis around for all the Playmates). That weekend was a no-go. So one day, I was shocked to get in the mail a save-the-date card announcing Joe's wedding. *Wedding?* I thought. I couldn't imagine him with just one girlfriend. I mean, look at Hef! And Joe was much younger and cuter. Still, from what I heard, Christina, his bride-to-be, was a really nice and normal pretty brunette who was an entertainment reporter.

I immediately booked our flights to Puerto Vallarta, a thirty-minute drive from Punta Mita, where Joe's mansion was located, and where the wedding was going to be held. Although some might think it inappropriate for a Catholic married mother of three to be friends with the Girls Gone Wild creator, I, however, argue that it can't be porn when several of the original actresses had accrued some college credits.

It was going to be an all-inclusive wedding, a three-day extravaganza that included free massages, Jet Skis, horseback riding, big themed parties, and all the alcohol we could drink. This was not a cash-bar wedding. It was a wedding with a twenty-four-hour personal concierge—everything was taken care of.

On our Alaska Airlines flight down there, I had my headphones on and was grooving out to rap music—songs about living the high life, drinking champagne, and hos, getting myself in the right mind-set. Peter nudged me. "We have to turn around and go back because a 747 was disabled on the runway in Puerto Vallarta."

"You're joking," I said as the lyric "Bitches be running their mouths," played out of my headset. However, I could tell by the other passengers, some of whom were also heading to the luxe wedding, that it was indeed true.

When we got back to LAX, one guy, who we referred to as Tall John, said he was trying to get us one of Joe's private planes to get us there. After drinking margaritas for two hours at the Gladstone's restaurant inside LAX, we finally realized Tall John was full of crap.

Since we already had a babysitter for the weekend, Peter

and I decided to splurge on a hotel room and get on another plane the next day. At two the following afternoon, Peter and I were in a taxi van on our way to the airport with two of Joe's three sisters and their husbands. Ten minutes into the ride, Peter couldn't find his passport. I refused to let my irresponsible husband ruin *my* fun. We had the cab pull over so Peter could look through his bags—nada, it wasn't there. I ordered the cab to take Peter back to the hotel to search for his passport and take the rest of us to the airport so that we wouldn't miss the plane.

Some might think that it was unwifely of me to abandon my passportless husband and pursue my own pleasure-seeking weekend, but this is the man who, even upon the birth of his sons, never even spent one night curled up in an uncomfortable chair in the maternity ward like every single one of my friends' husbands did. In fact, the night I gave birth to Brandon, I had such a bad cough that the doctor prescribed some cough medicine. Peter decided he also had a cough and took a huge dose of the medicine. By the time I pushed Brandon out, Peter could barely stand and his eyes were rolling back into his head. They put a mirror to the side of me so I could witness the moment Brandon's head popped out from my vagina. Just as Brandon opened his eyes for the first time a nurse yelled, "Dad is going down, Dad is going down!" Suddenly, all the attention was on Peter as they seated him in a chair and made sure he was stable. Right after they cleaned Brandon up and handed him to Peter for my sister Shannon to take a picture of them, he handed the baby to Shannon and said, "I have to go home and sleep." When he finally got home, he crawled into our bed not remembering my mother was sleeping in our California King, since she was there to watch the kids. In my opinion, if the roles had been reversed, he would have dropped me off in the middle of the highway holding my suitcase.

Peter eventually found the passport in his suitcase thirty minutes later, hopped in another cab, and made it to the airport just in time. I was waiting at the gate, and upon seeing me Peter said, "Give me your cell phone. I left mine in the cab." I said, "You are un-fucking-believable," and handed over my cell. Then he said, "Give me a hundred dollars so that the cab driver will come back and give the phone to me." I said, and quite loudly may I add, "You really are so un-fucking-believable!" When Peter returned with his phone I was being really cold and bitchy and then he said, "Well, if this is the way you are going to be, then maybe I don't want to go at all." I forced myself to change my attitude like a light switch in order to salvage the little bit of the weekend we had left. I hate fighting, but I hate fighting on vacation more.

The worst fight Peter and I have had was over data roaming. We were in a different part of Mexico with all three kids and somehow after giving me explicit instructions on how to use my iPhone in a foreign country, I screwed it up and he discovered I had left the data-roaming feature on or some bullshit. I still don't understand. But we had one of our worst fights. In the middle of it I yelled, "Do you think Prince William and Kate would ever argue about data roaming? Then why are we?" When we got back to America, I called customer service for AT&T and tried to explain what happened between Peter and me and asked how I could pay the added charge so it would be eliminated from the monthly bill and Peter wouldn't see it and get upset again. The poor Southern customer service rep honestly thought I was going to get beat up and told me to get out while I still could, but only after she told me all about her second husband, who was a real son of a bitch and a good-for-nothing duck hunter. I have to say, it was the juiciest conversation I'd ever had with a customer service rep.

Anyway, when we finally arrived for Joe's wedding, we discovered that other people from our original flight didn't want to wait the whole day and miss out on any fun, so they'd taken a midnight flight to Guadalajara and rented cars and drove to Punta Mita. *Really?* I thought. All for a free massage? A curious pairing in a car were Lance Bass and Cheryl Tiegs, who had never even met before. I had always liked Cheryl and could see us bonding over makeup tips.

The first party was an all-white-themed one with what looked like Cirque du Soleil crossed with drag queens surrounding us on the beach. Kris and Bruce Jenner were there, so we mingled with them a lot. In defense of Joe's presumed reputation, all of the couples and guests in attendance were quite normal and very sweet, and some we met eventually became dear friends.

The following evening, the wedding happened. Instead of a priest or a justice of peace, the officiator was a high-powered Hollywood agent. The bride, Christina, came down the aisle in a gorgeous but simple white dress, and Joe sported a custom-made tux.

The Hollywood agent started out by saying we were not there for a marriage but instead a civil union because, per

Joe's request, he said until gays in general could be married, he would not observe a traditional wedding. Peter leaned over to me and said, "This is so brilliant. He got this girl to marry him without really marrying him."

Me and Joe Francis at Kim Kardashian's wedding.

Right when we got back to L.A., we made plans to have dinner with Joe and Christina in about three weeks' time on a Saturday. The Tuesday before our big Saturday-night plans, I e-mailed both Joe and Christina separately confirming the location and time. Christina wrote back right away and said, "I'm so sorry I can't join you, but maybe Joe would like to join you by himself." I thought that was odd, and I had really been looking forward to getting to know her better, seeing as she is an entertainment reporter. There was always the chance that she would want to do a feature on me and my ascending career at *Chelsea Lately*. Two hours later, Joe wrote back and said, "I'm so sorry that we can't join you, but Christina and I are having marital problems." I wrote him back and said, "No worries. I totally understand"—as if I did understand a crisis three weeks into a marriage. Doesn't that actually count as the honeymoon?

Less than two weeks later, they issued a joint statement, stating that after careful consideration and with great respect and admiration for each other, they had decided to end their civil union. When I told Peter, I asked him if he would return the heart-shaped waffle maker I'd just bought to Williams-Sonoma the next day. We did end up going out with Joe alone and driving around the block in his Cadillac SUV. It had been converted into a limousine with an amazing sound system and bulletproof windows. Besides an amusement park, it's the most fun I've ever had in a car—other than blue-balling, of course.

The next time I saw Christina was August 20, 2011, less than a year later. She was standing with a microphone among a crush of reporters and fans and young teenage girls holding up signs that read KIM AND KRIS FOREVER! We were in a bus that was transporting guests from a heavily secured parking lot up to the Montecito mansion draped in all its glory where Kim Kardashian's wedding to Kris Humphries was being held. Joe was the one who pointed Christina out while he was sitting next to me.

I got my invitation a tad late—like, four days before the wedding—even though I've known the Kardashians personally since 2005, but this was the event of the year. My best friend, Liz, was now working as director of creative development for Kardashian/Jenner Communications and she had pulled out all the stops to get me there. Admittedly, I had done a bang-up job portraying the Kardashians on *Chelsea Lately,* so I felt I earned my rightful spot.

Trying to book a hotel room around Montecito was about as impossible as getting a room at the Four Seasons in London for William and Kate's wedding. It was also too late for me to call my good friend Oprah to see if we could crash at her pad. I didn't want to be rude. She usually enjoys longer stays with me. The only room I could get was one for six hundred dollars, which normally would have gone for two hundred on a typical weekend. Cheap Peter suggested just driving home after the wedding. I told Cheap Peter, "If you'd like to drive home, you're welcome to. I, for one, will enjoy the king-size bed in a snore-free room."

Like Joe and Christina, Kim and Kris didn't make it until death, but they did make it two months—seventy-two days, to be exact.

Our next celebrity wedding was for a roadie for Crosby, Stills, & Nash. My friend Mindy was marrying her longtime boyfriend, Roy. During their courtship she had caught him cheating twice. One time at a birthday for a different girlfriend, he took a forkful of cake and sling-shot it at her head, destroying her sixty-dollar blowout. Mindy was so horrified at his behavior that she got up, apologized to the group, and told Roy they were leaving, then took his hand like a toddler having a tantrum at another kid's birthday party. However, it's a little more difficult to throw a two-hundred-pound drunken boyfriend into a passenger seat than it is to place a crying twenty-six-pound child into a car seat and leave.

At the outdoor wedding in Santa Barbara, Mindy stood holding her colorful bouquet, and Roy stumbled down the aisle wearing Oakley sunglasses and holding a Budweiser. The whole ceremony was less than ten minutes. I just remember that I-do's were included.

We were at a table of ten at the reception, and while we were having a conversation with a couple beside us, a man from across our table, who had been listening to us and whom we had never met said, "Wait a minute. Is your name Peter? I recognize you from photos. I think I was engaged to Patsy after you were."

As it turns out, Peter had been engaged to a woman named Patsy about a year before he met me. The most recently scorned ex told the table, "Did you know that you were number four and I was number five?" Jeez, I thought, how does one woman get a man to kneel down with a ring five times? It wasn't like she was Julia Roberts in *Runaway Bride*. I also decided that a woman like that must really know her way around a penis. She's also the kind of selfish woman who would never share those dick tricks with another woman.

For the rest of the night Peter and this guy compared war stories as I danced with the groom's roadie compadres. Roy and Mindy would eventually have two kids within two years and then he'd leave her for another woman.

I had to ask myself, Are Peter and I bad luck as wedding guests? Sure, everyone complains about our hour-and-a-half-long Catholic wedding ceremony, but we're still here. My fantasy is to renew our vows outside in our backyard with our Bellagio-esque water fountains playing to Andrea Bocelli's music. I would have a three-gown wedding (all made by Vera Wang): one for the ceremony, one for the dinner, and then a short slutty one for the dancing. Chuy would be the ringbearer and I'd have Chelsea, Sarah Colonna, Jen Kirkman, and Fortune Feimster as my bridesmaids (and Liz as the maid of honor). They would all be in navy, because in my opinion my boss looks the best and thinnest in navy. Of course, it would all be televised on an E! "Celebrity Renewal Wedding" special. A separate deal would be made with *In Touch* magazine for the photo rights.

17

THE SIXTY-FIVE-YEAR-OLD INTERN

Working with *Chelsea Lately* doesn't come without a certain amount of risk. For example, we typically have college interns helping us with production. They tend to be guys who claim to be straight but act very effeminate. Though, some do flirt with me and say that they have a thing for cougars. I am of course honored, but I mostly needle them to embrace their gayness. I mean, there's a reason you're a twenty-year-old college guy whose favorite show is *Chelsea Lately*.

There was one intern, however, who did take special interest in me. He was a very special intern—as in "afterschool special." He was a sixty-five-year-old man whom we called "The Sixty-Five-Year-Old Intern" because we are genius comedians. Chelsea was dating Ted Harbert, who was president of E! at the time. The Sixty-Five-Year-Old Intern, whose real name was George, happened to be Ted's good friend. Chelsea came to the writers' meeting and told us, "Hey, Ted's really good friend who used to run all of the top sitcoms in the 1980s and '90s is basically retired but his third wife just left him. He's very depressed and Ted thought being exposed to comedy writers again would really help him. None of your jobs are threatened; this is just temporary."

George would just sit in the morning writers' meeting taking notes and soaking in our weird ambiance. Then one day he piped up, "What about doing a parody of *Sgt. Bilko?*" To which we all said, "Interesting. Who is that?" George replied, "You're kidding. It was a hit sitcom that ran on CBS from 1955 to 1959." We politely laughed, as in addition to being genius comics we are smart enough to know not to piss on the friend of the network's president.

Early on, George asked if he could come to my office and watch me work on my jokes for the show. Again, recognizing that I like my paycheck, I said "Sure. That'll be fun." My office is small, so he had to sit on my big yoga ball, which he had trouble balancing on because he'd just had hip-replacement surgery. Halfway through writing the jokes, a production assistant delivered my Chinese chicken salad that I have every day and that I pay for. George said to the PA, "Oh, I'll have one of those too." She said, "They're nine dollars," and he just said, "Oh, never mind." Knowing that seniors should eat every few hours, I offered half of my salad to him, which he happily accepted. As is typical for me, we got right into his personal life. His first wife he cheated on, his second wife cheated on him, and his third wife's career as a doctor specialist/TV personality was just starting to take off and she tired of him.

By the third day of sharing my nine-dollar lunch with him, which he never offered me $4.50 for, he said that the house he owns now was Kate Hudson's childhood home. With my knowledge of real estate, I calculated that it was definitely worth more than $5 million when he told me what part of L.A. it was located in. I looked down at my half salad and thought, Heather, why are you sharing your meal with a multimillionaire?

My office was becoming stuffy, and I figured out that I was the only one dealing with him. The woman I was sharing my office with was going away for a week, so George said, "Great, then I'll just set up shop here for the week." He added, "I love being on a diet with you and only eating a half Chinese chicken salad. I've already lost a couple of pounds. But next time, can you order half the amount of wonton crunchies?"

Later, I was in Chelsea's office, and I said, "Do you know that George plans on spending the entire week in my office while Lisa's gone?" Chelsea was excited. She said, "Oh that's great. I'm so glad you two are getting along. I'll have to tell Ted." And I said, "No, Chelsea, besides him taking half my lunch, I provide therapy for him, not only for his last wife but for his thirty-year-old son who he had a rift with regarding a property in Vermont that he had put a lien against. Technically, at thirty, he thought his son should be responsible enough to handle these matters. And to tell you the truth, I agree with George." Chelsea seemed bored with what I was talking about. She said, "Let me talk to Ted."

The next day, our executive producer came to our meeting and said, "The Sixty-Five-Year-old Intern will no longer be returning, being that he is not currently enrolled in a four-year university." I thought, Great, I can eat again, but part of me missed him. I actually shared the Sergent Bilko jokes with my eighty-year-old father; I had never seen him laugh so hard. But he isn't exactly our ideal demographic.

Another occupational hazard that comes with working for Chelsea Handler is that your personal life can suffer, and sometimes you aren't even aware that it is suffering. This was the case when I experienced a very bizarre weekend at home. That Saturday morning I was at my son's T-ball game alone with all three of my kids because on Saturday mornings Peter goes golfing. This was when one of the single mothers who religiously watches *Chelsea Lately* sat down next to me. Her name was Katy, and she asked me, "How is everything going?"

"Oh fine . . . Brandon, don't climb the chain-link fence!" I yelled at my three-year-old, who was edging toward the top of the batting cage.

"It's hard doing everything by yourself. But I wouldn't have it any other way. I'm so much happier now," she said.

"That's great and very brave of you. It's important to be happy. You can't be a good mother if you're miserable in your relationship," I said, reassuring her.

"You're brave too," she said.

"Thanks," I said.

At this point I thought she was referring to the previous night's sketch where I once again appeared in a one-piece bathing suit.

"Hey, a few of my divorced girlfriends, we call ourselves the Double D's for Divorced Divas—get it? You can use that in your act if you want. We're going to the Sagebrush Cantina in Calabasas tonight at seven o'clock for men and margaritas, which we call M&M's, get it? You can use that in your act too if you want. Do you think you can get your mom to watch the kids so you can join us?" she asked.

Sagebrush has been a major cheesy Valley scene for the past two decades, but I hadn't been there since *Chelsea Lately* started to air and figured a few people may recognize me from the show, so I decided to go. I knew I would get a lot more attention if I could somehow convince Chelsea to join me, but the only thing that irritates Chelsea more than drunk Valley cougars are drunk and married Valley cougars. So before I agreed to join them, I made it clear that my blond star was out of town performing that weekend, which Katy seemed to accept without disappointment.

"Actually, Peter can watch the kids," I said.

"Wow, that's great. It's really important to keep the lines of communication open, especially when it comes to the kids," she said.

I thought that was kind of an odd comment to make about someone's marriage whom you've just met but I said, "Yes, always. I'll see you there." Then I uncurled Brandon's fingers off the chain-link fence.

When I arrived at the Sagebrush Cantina that night, I quickly found Katy and the other Double D's. They all told me I could use them in my act several slurred times, along with how they all believed Chelsea and them were so much alike that they would be best friends. One of the women,

Sue, though heterosexual her entire forty-one years on this earth, was now seeing a woman romantically for the first time. I always find it interesting that a woman can be married and leave her husband for another woman and then go back to men, just like Melissa Etheridge's first wife, Julie, left Lou Diamond Phillips for her. Being that I am a fan of lesbianism, I began to ask a million questions. Why do lesbians use strap-ons? If they are truly lesbians, shouldn't they be able to get off with the parts God gave them? You never hear about gay guys strapping on breasts when they have sex with each other. I wasn't comfortable asking that out loud, but I did ask "How did it happen? . . . Do you take turns or can you get away with just receiving? . . . Do you take a lot of baths together like when Kim Cattrall was a lesbian for two episodes in season five of *Sex and the City*?" I was then interrupted by Katy, who said, "Heather, shouldn't you know these things?"

"I guess at this point in my life and career I should," I joked.

Then Sue stood up and took my hand and declared, "We're dancing!"

I agreed and headed to the dance floor. Besides, I thought, people would be more likely to recognize me on the dance floor than tucked away in a booth. Sue started really dancing with me, squatting down before me, then running her hands up my legs while coming back up, all the while keeping eye contact. It was your typical "Let's pretend we're lesbians dancing so we get more attention from the guys" dance. But I was feeling a little uncomfortable. Thank God that during the '90s, when I was hitting the clubs with my friends, we weren't expected to make out with each other just for a free round of drinks. By the end of the song I'd had enough of Sue rubbing her ass up against my vagina and flipping her blond hair extensions in my face, so I did the universal sign language for "I'm getting another drink," and headed back to our table.

As the women got even more intoxicated and no one was approaching our table except to take our order, I decided to call it a night. I surmised the Valley wasn't watching E! Maybe they all had to cancel their cable due to the recession. I figured, Why should I sit here and waste any more calories on chips and salsa?

The next morning was Sunday, and I took the kids to our Catholic church for Mass. It can be a challenge, especially when Drake whines that Mass takes too long, to which I calmly respond, "Oh really? Well, Jesus Christ was nailed to a cross for three hours in the blazing-hot sun and died there for your sins, so the least you can do in return is sit an air-conditioned room for one hour." But because my three-year-old boy likes to climb on the statues of the saints at each station of the cross, we have to go into the small room to the right of the altar with soundproof glass off the main church. It has been dubbed the Crying Room for good reason: the kids and the parents are crying when they're in it. There I saw my good friend Anna, whose son is Drake's best friend. I smiled at her and she smiled back with very sad eyes. When Mass ended, we headed out to the auditorium, where the doughnuts were sold. There is nothing like using a baked good with roughly twenty-nine grams of sugar to bribe your kid to put his palms together and pray. As Brandon was touching all twelve doughnuts in the box before deciding on the chocolate with rainbow sprinkles, Anna approached me.

"Heather, how are you?" she said as she hugged me and rocked me back and forth.

"I'm fine. How are you?" I asked.

"So can you still come with the boys to our cabin next weekend or won't you have them?" she asked as she touched her diamond crucifix on her neck.

"Yes, we're coming, but with traffic on Friday night Peter thought it would be better if we came up early on Saturday morning instead," I said.

"You're coming together, both you and Peter, are you sure?" she said as she tilted her head to one side.

"Yes, he can skip golf one Saturday morning. Of course he is coming. Why are you acting so weird?" I asked.

"Because your Facebook status says you're single, and even though I'm a Catholic Republican, I don't care if you are gay or confused or feel you need to find yourself in the arms of another woman. My God loves everyone, and it won't change our friendship."

In that split second it hit me. The moment when I left my desk on Friday to get Chelsea another blended margarita, I had left her alone in my office for approximately four minutes—just enough time for her to change my Facebook status.

"Oh my God, Chelsea got on my computer and changed my Facebook status. Peter and I are fine," I said.

"So if you and Peter are still together, what about you being bisexual? How does Peter feel about that?" she asked.

"I'm not bisexual, Anna!" I yelled, then quickly remembered we were on parish property, so I lowered my voice. "Anna, Chelsea must have changed my sexual preference too."

It all made perfect sense—everything including Katy and horny Sue thinking I was single and bi-curious.

When I got home I immediately logged on and went to my profile page and changed my relationship status, and who I was interested in, back to Married, and Friends. Then I discovered the most horrifying part. My birth date now read June 14, 1964. That bitch didn't just make me a cougar; she made me a gray panther! As if I needed to be any older than I already am. I started reading the messages and wall postings from the previous two days. One was from my friend's ex-boyfriend asking if I wanted to talk; one from a friend's current husband; and one was from Alecia Powell, who was in my class at my all-girl high school but came as Alex Powell to the ten-year reunion. Then there were some posts that were so vulgar from creepy male fans that I had to defriend them.

So the valuable lesson learned from all of this is to always press Control, Alt, Delete on your computer when Chelsea Handler is in the building.

18

CRAIGSLISTING FOR FAMILY POOL PARTIES

We bought the ranch house next door to my parents in 2005. I knew we were ready to move from our old place when I was at Toys "R" Us looking at play kitchens to buy Mackenzie and they were nicer and more up-to-date than our kitchen at home. L.A. real estate is very expensive, which can be frustrating when I'd be watching *Oprah* about a family who was in terrible debt and only made $14,000 a year, yet when they showed their kitchen it was three times the size of mine and had a huge island and new appliances. We were able to afford the house next to my parents because it was in terrible shape, but had a lot of land so we could add on and remodel it. It was also very convenient because my parents' house had a big, beautiful pool and Jacuzzi, and our house didn't come with either. Sure, it can be a little awkward when we have pool parties and don't invite my parents, but they seem very content watching us frolic away in the water from their living-room window.

On one particularly hot July day, my husband had invited Tom, a guy he met golfing, and his family, thinking we would really hit it off because his wife, Nancy, and I had gone to the same high school, but a few years apart, so we didn't know each other.

When they arrived, the first surprise was that there were five of them, and not four. Peter had golfed with this guy several times, spending hours with him, but told me they only had two children. Oh, guys and details, what's a third kid? The children quickly got into my parents' pool as Peter and I did. But Nancy and Tom just sat there sweating in the blazing sun fully clothed. Peter asked, "Don't you want to come in?" Tom replied with great surprise, "We've never been to a pool party where the parents swim too, so we didn't bring our suits."

I said to Nancy, "Would you like to borrow one of my bikinis?" But she gave me a horrified look like I was a swinger and she could catch a venereal disease from my suit. She said, "No, that's all right," and drove all the way home to get her suit and Tom's. By the time she came back I was already on my second lemonade and vodka, which is simply the best drink to have because on a really hot day when you're swimming-pool drinking, you need an alcoholic beverage with ice to keep it cold.

Nancy and I were not hitting it off. She bragged that every night all three of her children were asleep by six thirty p.m. I couldn't fathom it. The only way I could get my children to sleep at that hour was if I put Ambien in their ice cream, which I have never done because I don't have a prescription for Ambien.

Luckily, the kids were getting along in the pool. As I got up to get another drink, Nancy said, "My, you're having another?" I replied, "Well, it's not as though the kids can't swim. Besides, Peter's here and he was actually a lifeguard in San Diego." We continued on and had a cookout while my parents, Bob and Pam, looked out their bay window, waving. By six, I was feeling rather buzzed but I figured Tom and Nancy would be leaving because the kids had to hit the hay by six thirty. But Tom was having such a good time that every time Nancy encouraged him to leave, he waved her away and continued to drink beers with Peter.

Nancy decided to pick up the conversation a bit, so she told me how she loved to scrapbook. (The only photos of my children are on my iPhone.) She explained how she was an independent distributor for Creative Memories, selling photo-safe scrapbook albums. As she went on and on about being a memory manager, my eyeballs started to slope downward and I kept having to electric shock myself awake. I would say, "Now, explain this better. How I can cut photos into perfectly shaped hearts with the custom cutting system?" Then I could count on Nancy for a good ten-minute wrap-up.

We were soon approaching seven o'clock and I desperately wanted to take a nap. I looked in on the playroom at our place, and her kids had boundless energy, which convinced me even more that she was putting Ambien in their bedtime milk. For an hour as we sat outside in our backyard, Nancy had moved on to how much she loved Pandora charm bracelets and proceeded to tell me the story behind every charm that Tom had bought for her on special holidays. There was one called Forever Together, Wanda's Garden, and well, I just blacked out until she told me she and Tom were also planning on spending a little alone time on an upcoming Pandora Cruise, which advertises "Unforgettable Memories Together." Now, if she would have been an independent consultant for Passion Parties, where they sell sex toys, we might have had more in common, but this was simply not working. By eight, Nancy and I were watching the children in the playroom. I was lying down on the couch as she sat in a chair beside me. She was babbling on about how she bought a dress at her friend's house, which was in a different pyramid—excuse me, I meant to say multilevel marketing scheme—for Cabi Clothes and how embarrassed she was that following Sunday when eight other women in her parish sported the same dress. That's about the last thing I remember before I was passed out in my son's Pixar *Cars* Steve McQueen mini chair with Nancy next to me still going on about getting in on the ground floor of something.

I was startled back to semiconsciousness by Nancy as she shook me, screaming, "Heather! Heather! Peter, call 911, there's something wrong with Heather!" Both Tom and Peter came into the room and Drake said out loud, "Nothing's wrong with Mommy. She just gets sleepy from her lemonade." No sooner than that, Tom and Nancy were packing up their sleep-deprived children (as it was now eight thirty) and heading out our door. Tom said he would call Peter to play golf, and I shouted to Nancy, "Send me a brochure on the cruise! It sounds like one charm of a trip."

If Nancy had a problem with me being drunk in my own home, she would have gone apeshit over the situation Peter and I found ourselves in a couple weeks later. A fellow school parent, Brady, offered to drive us to a party to watch a boxing match on pay per view at a mutual friend's home. We didn't have any pregnant friends at the time and we were so happy that we could go to a party and drink without having to drive, because that responsibility would fall on our designated driver, Brady. It never occurred to us that Brady did the majority of his drinking before getting behind the wheel.

Peter and I hopped into the minivan, and because there was a car seat, I had to sit in the middle next to Peter, while Brady's wife sat in the front. We had to go through a canyon to get to the party, which is when we realized how drunk Brady truly was. Brady was speeding up and passing slower cars on a two-lane road. I was more worried about embarrassing him and telling him to slow the fuck down than for my own safety. Because of where I was sitting, I had no air bag. Peter had one, as did Brady and his wife.

Thankfully we eventually got to the party without any maiming. But the first chance we had, I pulled Peter aside and said, "I don't care if we have to take a cab home, we are not traveling back with them. Do you realize I could have gone through that window if there was an accident? I'd never work in TV again!" Peter said, "Actually, I was calculating the maximum amount of insurance he might have had, and divided that by four people. Your portion would not have been enough to put you back together. How would I even work if I had to push you around in a wheelchair all day?" I gave him a death stare. "Really? You do realize you added up math calculations and not once spoke of your love for me. I think you need to go out and get me a diamond Pandora bracelet with a charm of a car."

After we got safely home via taxi from the party, we took an inventory of our friends with kids and realized the list was shortening. We just wanted to party with a couple like us, and who were honest about who they were.

I didn't want a hypocrite like the mother at my preschool who preaches against vaccinating our children, insisting on a nondairy, and all-organic gluten-free diet and yet left her baggie of cocaine in a prescription bottle with her name on it in the bathroom during a PTA meeting. I thought coke addicts were supposed to be less scattered and more on top of things like Charlie Sheen in the original *Wall Street* movie. Besides, my kids don't eat that bad. In fact, they're quite sophisticated. The other day they requested truffle oil on their French fries. But that's when I thought that maybe we could list our friendship needs on Craigslist. The ad would read:

> *Married heterosexual couple with children aged four to ten looking for pool-party friends with similar-aged children who can swim without floaties, to share good times. Parents must enjoy meat and regular grocery-store-bought foods, and like to day-drink beer, wine, or vodka on the weekends. No drugs or smoking; however, cigars welcome. No swingers. Family must live within a fifteen-mile radius and have a pool to reciprocate. Golf and no scrapbooking a plus.*

19

BAD WORD

When Peter calls me and says, "Hey, the school called and . . ." a lot races through my brain. But I admit the one thing that never pops into my brain is Drake/Mackenzie/Brandon will be awarded Student of the Year. So on one occasion Peter continued, "Drake was caught trying to sell a bad word for two dollars." Yes, just like you, that was the first time in my life that I ever heard of anyone trying to sell a word for cash. I've heard of cash for gold, and in the case of my single friend Tara, gold for Botox when she was so desperate to remove an expression line from her forehead that she traded a gold bracelet an ex-boyfriend had given her for 60 cc of the good stuff.

According to the teacher who called Peter, Drake and his friend Evan, while in the classroom, were overheard telling another boy if he wanted to know the new bad word, he'd have to pay two dollars. The teacher sent all three to the vice principal's office, where each was questioned separately. Drake and Evan were given a slip of paper for their parents to sign saying they used inappropriate language. The third boy did not get the slip at all. Maybe because he didn't have any money and therefore the word transaction was never officially closed.

I asked Peter as I was driving home, "Well, what was the word?" Peter took a deep sigh and said, "It was 'nigga.' Not 'nigger,' but 'nigga,' with an *a* at the end. According to the vice principal, Evan heard it in a rap song and told Drake about it." I was appalled. "Let me talk to Drake alone when I get home," I said, and I disconnected my Bluetooth in my car and let my hip-hop radio station continue. I thought, How did Evan even hear the word? It must have been from Evan's older brother, who was in eighth grade. I continued to listen to one of my favorite tunes, DMX's "Party Up," and couldn't help but sing along in my operatic voice, *"Y'all gon' make me lose my mind up in here up in here . . . Y'all gon' make me act a fool up in here up in here . . ."*

I admit I listen to hip-hop music all the time. I always loved it, even before I started working with the Wayans brothers. I adore hearing about the ghetto and the LBC, short for Long Beach County, which despite being a beach community seems a little rough. However, the only time listening to hip-hop music caused me trouble was when I accidentally pulled over thinking a cop was behind me, but it was actually just the police sirens they like to lay over the tracks to make you feel like you really in da hood just tryin' to make a dolla' to feed your daughter. I admit I was never one of those moms who played Disney CDs in my car when the kids were with me. I always played popular music. Sometimes it's cute when Brandon sings a Justin Bieber song in perfect pitch, but other times it's not as cute, like when he was coloring a picture of Jack and Jill in day care and just started singing, *"Roll up, wait a minute, let me put some kush up in it."*

After dinner I took Drake into his room to talk about the word. I said to him, "Now, Drake, tell me exactly what happened today at school."

"Well, first of all we were never going to charge our friend. That was just a joke. I never would have made him pay me the two dollars," he said as his eyes widened.

"The money is not the issue here, Drake, it's the word. Tell me how you heard the word," I demanded.

"Evan saw it on his older brother's computer when he was downloading a song off iTunes. It was in the title of the song, and Evan told me it was bad," he answered.

"So what did you think it meant?" I asked.

"I thought it meant something like the F word or the S-H word. But now I know what it means because the vice principal told me," he said.

"And what does it mean?" I continued.

"The word is used when you're being mean to African Americans," he said.

"Yes, that is true," I said.

Drake got an inquisitive look on his face and asked, "But why do people sing songs about being mean to African Americans?"

I knew I had to answer, but in a way that a nine-year-old could understand, so I said, "Look, some African American artists like to use that word in their rap songs and they believe it is OK, and it is not being mean because *they* are African Americans. But since you are a Caucasian American—"

Drake interrupted, "What is Caucasian?"

"It's another word for white," I said as I tried to continue.

"Then why wouldn't you just say white?" he questioned.

"Fine. Because you are white, you can never, ever, ever say that word, sing it, or write it down. That is the law, and depending on what state you get caught saying it in, the punishment can vary but it's always very bad especially if you're a comedian and you say it onstage and someone videotapes you saying it. Even if you were on the number-one-rated sitcom for more than a decade, you will be dead in this town, you got it?" Drake just shook his head yes.

The next morning at work I was telling the other writers and our executive producer, Tom, the N-word story and I told them what I said later that night as I put Drake to bed. I said, "Drake, I'm going to tell you another word that is just as bad, if not worse, than the N word, and that word is 'fag.' " Tom interrupted me and said, "Looks like Drake just found a way to make another two dollars." Everyone burst into laughter. It's so annoying, these childless people have no idea what I go through; they're just waiting to get their next joke in. What I wanted to say before I was so rudely interrupted by the assholes I work with is that I told Drake that the F-A-G word, which fortunately he had never heard before, was a word used to be mean to gay people. I said, "And you know there is nothing wrong with someone if they fall in love with someone of the same sex. You never make fun of them for that." Then Drake rolled his eyes and said, "Of course there is nothing wrong with being gay. Hello, I watch *Modern Family,* duh." I felt so relieved that at least I was doing something right. Drake had never gotten in trouble before and had certainly never been accused of being a bully or saying mean things.

That night I was talking to my gay book agent, the same gay book agent Chelsea constantly refers to and features on the show. Michael is great and he really cares about his clients. At the time, he was upset that the publisher hadn't changed the font on the cover of my book for me to approve yet so he said, "If they don't change that cheap-looking font by Tuesday, I'm going to go full faggot on them!" Now, in that case I don't think I need to explain that some gay men of a certain age can use the word if it means getting their literary client the response they deserve. I felt it was just best that Drake knows never to say the N word, whether it ends in *er* or in *a* and also never to use the F word, whether it ends in *uck* or *ag.*

That weekend, Evan's dad took the boys to see *Red Tails,* about the all–African American flight squadron in World War II. The next day we rented *The Help* and watched it twice. Both of these movies seemed to make a strong impression on Drake. I felt pretty good about everything until he saw *White Chicks,* where Marlon and Shawn Wayans play two African American FBI agents who have to pose as shallow white female socialites to solve a crime in the Hamptons, on TV. When I appeared as the saleswoman in the movie, Drake for once seemed to be impressed. So I explained how I had worked for the Wayans brothers on other TV shows and movies. I said, "Yes, Drake, the black man has been very good to me and to a few of my close girlfriends."

20

DOES MY BOY LIKE BARBIE?

Since my kids go to the same Catholic elementary school that I attended, parent-teacher conferences can be interesting. The classroom still smells the same and even some of my old teachers are still there. But I still learn something new every time I visit, like, it's never a good sign when the teacher starts the meeting with a mandatory prayer. When I met with Drake's second-grade teacher in the fall, everything seemed to be right on track in terms of his reading and math skills, but then she said, "I do want to share a concern I have with you regarding Drake's self-portrait." She pulled out a large piece of paper with what looked like a girl. "That is Drake's self-portrait? But that's a little girl." She sighed. "Exactly, that's my concern. We asked all the children to draw themselves in crayon and your son's came out like this." The picture had a little girl with blond pigtails and brown eyes, wearing a red dress. The teacher continued, "Have you heard of gender-identity crisis?"

"Yes, but I don't think Drake has that. I don't even think he's gay, and I'm very open to that. In fact, every time we're at Target I say to him 'Drake, would you like a Barbie or My Little Pony? If you do, I'll buy it for you because it's OK.' But every time he says no. And he refuses to wear pink, no matter how hard I try."

"Well, this little girl is wearing red. Does Drake like red?" she countered.

I said, "I've seen the kids on *Oprah* where their parents allow them to dress like the opposite sex at a very young age or even change their name. I applaud Angelina and Brad for letting Shiloh dress like Ellen DeGeneres. I was the first to call it at *Chelsea Lately* when Shiloh was only eighteen months old. She was photographed wearing an old pair of Maddox's army boots and I said to the other writers, 'Mark my word, Shiloh is a lesbian and she is going to make some woman very happy someday with those genes.'"

The teacher just stared at me. So I said, "Anyway, thank you for bringing it to my attention. I'll talk to Drake about it."

I was beginning to get a little worried, and I couldn't help but wonder whether this had anything to do with the fact that I didn't breastfeed Drake. Did he want to be a girl because he never got the chance to suck on a boob? That night I showed Peter Drake's self-portrait and explained the teacher's concern. "Peter, I remember watching an old episode of Sonny and Cher, and Cher joked at the end of the show that Chastity hated wearing dresses. I don't want to be Cher. I mean, of course I would love to be Cher and perform at Caesars Palace with my scary face-lift. Who wouldn't want to retire in Las Vegas? You could golf like Celine Dion's husband, René, and then I would perform at night."

Peter interrupted, "What are you talking about? Get to the point."

I took a deep breath. "My point is that if Drake is a Chaz Bono, I don't want him to wait until forty to be who he believes he is. I want him to be on *Dancing with the Stars* way before that!" I exclaimed.

"Look, he probably just didn't understand the assignment and got distracted. Can I just sleep?" Peter begged.

I crawled into Drake's bed that night like I do every night to tell him a made-up story. I told him the story of a little girl whose mother was on TV. The child was embarrassed by it and never really felt comfortable in the skin she was born in. The little girl hated wearing matching sequin-and-feather dresses with her mother despite the fact that they were designed by the one and only Bob Mackie, and then Drake interrupted me and asked, "Is this another story about you and us being embarrassed about what you do on *Chelsea Lately*? Because I like it better when you make up a completely new story." Oh my God, I thought. He is relating to the Cher and Chastity story. I finally asked him, "Honey, do you ever wish you were born a little girl instead of a little boy?" Drake ignored my question and demanded, "You have to tell me another story. That one sucked." I was so tired from worrying about this self-portrait, I couldn't come up with another story and I said, "Drake, I can't tonight. You know I work very hard. I'm on two shows." And he retorted, "Yeah, but *Chelsea Lately* and *After Lately* are from the same company, so it doesn't really count as two shows. Just tell me a story and please make it funny this time." I continued, "You know, Drake, it's tiring for me. Imagine if after playing two baseball games I forced you to go to batting practice at nine at night?" Drake sighed and said, "Oh please, you don't even work out, you just sit at a computer, it's not that hard. Now, tell the story." Well, whatever he is, Drake's a manipulative little shit who knows how to get his way. At least that will get him far in life, whether he grows up to be a man or a woman.

I decided not to share this latest dilemma with my parents. I just didn't think they'd get it, especially since the last time they came over, Mackenzie was busy putting the boys in her old Easter dresses. They ended up doing an entire fashion show for my dad. Of course, this never-before-seen runway couture show had to take place when my very conservative, traditional parents were present. I immediately demanded that the boys change and start wrestling and beating the shit out of each other like normal, so my dad could witness their male aggression.

The Saturday after the self-portrait talk, Drake and the rest of the second-graders at St. Ignatius were receiving their Sacrament of Reconciliation, otherwise known as First Holy Confession, where for the first time as Catholics, they confess their sins to a priest. Nowadays, at least at our parish, they do it on the altar, where the parents can see their child tell the priest face-to-face what their sins are. I assume they do it this way to put everyone's mind at ease that their kid is not going into a dark room with a pedophile priest. From where the parents were, none of us could hear what our children were confessing.

Afterward, we had a little coffee and doughnut reception. Lisa Sights, a fellow second-grade mother, came up to me and said, "I saw you on TV last night." Normally, nothing would make me happier than knowing that some of these nerd parents are actually watching my show. However, my heart stopped because the episode she was referring to involved a sketch in which I went to Chippendales in Las Vegas. In the sketch, after I give one of the dancers a lap dance, Sarah Colonna "accidentally" rips off my dress, leaving me in just a nude strapless bra and panties. Then, in front of a live audience, the Chippendales dancer I had just been grinding on lifts me up over his completely shaven and well-oiled chest, and carries me offstage.

Lisa Sights has no filter. She went on to explain to all of us how funny it was to see me standing there practically naked and then being carried off by such a hunky guy. Panicking, I tried to cut her off. "If we didn't have a big ending like that, our executive producer was going to kill the shoot altogether, and since I had already secured a free dinner at Eva Longoria's restaurant and Peter and I were going to make a whole Las Vegas weekend out of it, complete with Celine Dion concert tickets set for the following night, it would be the one time I wouldn't mind someone mistaking me for her, so I couldn't say no and had to agree to having my dress ripped off on film." But it was too late. I saw the other parents' uncomfortable faces as they rested their palms on their children's ears to keep their now-clean souls from hearing about the way this married mother of three is forced to make a living. I looked over to my right and saw that Drake had left my side and was running outside to play in the yard. I tried to save myself by awkwardly adding, "I don't let Drake watch *Chelsea Lately*. You know, you really need to monitor what your kids watch these days."

That night as I relaxed in bed next to Drake we talked about him receiving his sacrament. Somehow I got him to tell me what he confessed to the priest. He said, "Well, I said how I hit Brandon sometimes just because I feel like it and then . . . never mind."

"No, Drake, tell me. No matter what, I'm not going to be mad," I said.

"OK, but you promise not to tell my teacher?" he begged.

"OK, I promise," I said.

"I told the priest how I cheated in school, but just on, like, one thing, and it wasn't even really cheating because it wasn't math or spelling, it was art," he said.

"How do you cheat at art?" I asked.

"We were told to draw something, but as the teacher was explaining it, my mind wandered and I started thinking about Black Hawks on my Xbox, so I was afraid to ask because she gets mad when I don't listen. So I copied what Emma was drawing. I didn't think it was a big deal because it was just a picture of a girl, but then the teacher said she had to hold on to it. I don't know if she knows I copied it or not. I just wanted God to know and forgive me."

Well, there you go. My son didn't suffer from gender-identity issues, he was just a cheater with possible ADD. Once again Peter smugly said, "Well, of course it was something like that. I was never worried. God, why do you make such a big deal out of things?"

"It's called being a parent who cares," I said. I got into bed and just as Peter's breath started to get heavier but before an audible snort, I said, "Do you think he's going to be the kind of kid who would cheat on a high school entrance exam? Because a boy did that in my eighth grade and he ended up having to go to a public high school and no one has ever heard from him again." Peter said, "God, will you just let me sleep for once?"

Last week for the first time Drake told me he liked a girl in his class named Missy. He pointed her out to me in the school play. She was quite cute—a thin, blond, blue-eyed girl who could actually sing. I'm not surprised by Drake's type, since Emily was his all-time favorite Bachelorette. Sometimes I fantasize about Drake one day being the Bachelor, but then I worry because he is such a picky eater. What would he eat at the hometown dates? He'd insult every girl's family. I voiced this thought at a writers' meeting, where all but two writers screamed, "He'd eat four servings of pussy!" Seriously, I work with these people. But I can't imagine what I would do if I didn't like my son's girlfriend, which is why I'm still secretly hoping he might be gay. That way, I'd be the only woman in his life forever. Some would argue it's not healthy for a mother to tell her sons things like "No woman will ever love you as much as I do." Or constantly ask them in my singsong voice, "Who is the prettiest mommy who ever lived?" I disagree. To me that's just positive parenting for the mother and the child. I'm sorry, but I fear that some woman will break their heart with their Venus fly trap of a vagina.

When I think about my boys dating, I often remember a story my sister Shannon told me about a client she was defending for a DUI. He had received a full scholarship to UCLA, but right before he was about to settle into his all-expenses-paid dorm room he met a twenty-year-old single mother of two, fell in love, and decided to instead get a job and move in with her. She then got pregnant with his baby, or so he thought, until the baby came out very black. Once it was confirmed that the baby's father was their next-door neighbor, he started drinking a lot and was subsequently arrested for driving under the influence. His poor parents! At least if my son were gay, his boyfriend couldn't trap him with a pregnancy that wasn't even his. But for now I try not to worry about who my boys will fall in love with and just try to enjoy the little things, like the fact that they are not cheating in art class anymore.

How do I know Drake is no longer cheating in art class, you may ask? Well, at our school, they offer to make Christmas cards out of your child's original artwork for you to send to family and friends. I signed up Drake for two dozen cards without looking at his drawing. This was negligent on my part. When I got the cards, Drake insisted that we send all twenty-four out. I would have been excited if this particular Drake original wasn't a drawing of a Christmas tree with one boy shooting another smaller boy and red blood splattering over wrapped presents. Hey, at least he drew himself as a male, so merry Christmas, everyone, from our family to yours.

21

OMELET

After a couple years of marital bliss with her husband, Michael Goldstein, my sister Shannon decided to go off the pill and try to become pregnant. Michael really is a perfect husband. He is Jewish but told my mother that when they have kids that they could be raised Catholic because Shannon is a much better Catholic than he is a Jew; besides, Jesus was a Jew and a total babe—just look at his abs! Forget about the Situation, what about the Crucifixion? My mother always told us Jews made the best husbands because they loved to give their wives jewelry! She adores Michael as a son-in-law, and anytime she meets someone Jewish, the next thing out of her mouth is, "My daughter married a Jew and couldn't be happier. Now she's Shannon Clare McDonald Goldstein." As if the person thinks what a nice Christian she is for letting her daughter marry one of them, how liberal of her. My mom's "positive racism," as I like to refer to it, would come out when she'd be trying to sell a house to a potential buyer who is African American. He would come in and she'd strike up the conversation by saying, "Oh, are you a professional athlete?" And if he said no, she'd continue with, "You must be in the music industry." In one case the man answered, "No, I'm an ER doctor." And my mom's face lit up and she said, "Do you know Dr. Keith Black? He's an internationally renowned neurosurgeon at Cedars-Sinai. His name is Black but he is black too." When the doctor told my mom he did not know Dr. Black, my mom said, "Well, you should meet him, you'd really hit it off." Let me make it clear that my mother has never met Dr. Black herself. She has only read about him in the *L.A. Times,* and therefore thought he was brilliant, and quite handsome, and not just for a black man but for a doctor in general.

I knew Shannon had Michael pussy-whipped when he said to me in all seriousness, "Your sister makes the best shrimp cocktail." I said, "Not to take anything away from Shannon's culinary skills, but you do realize that all she has to do is buy the peeled shrimp and open a jar of shrimp cocktail sauce and the dish is done?" And he said, "Yes, but it's the way she does it that is just so amazing."

Shannon and Michael started trying to get pregnant about a year and half in, but nothing sprouted. So Shannon decided to see a fertility doctor. As directed by her doctor, Shannon gave herself shots in her butt cheek and boned her husband on the certain days when the doctor had calculated she was ovulating. During these times, she was also instructed to place pillows under her butt while holding her legs straight up in the air for an hour after sex. By the way, single ladies, if you ever want to really freak out a one-night stand, after you have sex with him, wait for him to return from the bathroom and then have him find you with your legs straight up in the air with pillows propped under you, and then just say to him, "Don't worry, the doctor says I only need to do this for an hour after. I just think you'd make such a wonderful father and provider."

The treatments eventually got more invasive, with Shannon's husband having to masturbate into a cup so she could be artificially inseminated. After that failed several times, she moved into in-vitro, where they would extract her eggs from her ovaries and then fertilize them with Michael's sperm in a Petri dish, and then they'd choose the strongest-looking embryos to put back inside her uterus, and freeze the other embryos in a super-size Sub-Zero fridge to use in the future.

Shannon was still not pregnant. She always got her results around four p.m. and when my phone would ring, my heart would drop as she'd say, her voice cracking, "It didn't work. I'm not pregnant." Shannon began to try any alternative methods she could get her hands on, like acupuncture. Besides having to drive two hours to have some strange Chinese guy poke needles in her, he also instructed her to drink this tea that looked like dirt from my backyard, which she had to make in a special teapot, not just any teapot. After driving to five different stores she finally found the teapot and drank the dirt tea, but still no pregnancy. She and Michael even considered going to Hawaii, where you're supposed to bone on some rock shaped like a huge penis to get pregnant. They were ready to buy their plane tickets when Shannon heard from a friend who'd got pregnant two years earlier on the rock. She had just filed for divorce, and that made Shannon more superstitious about why *not* to bone on the rock.

In the meantime, I got pregnant with Drake and a few months after he was born Shannon called me after she visited her fertility doctor and said, "I don't know what we are going to try next, but Dr. Paulson did bring up the possibility of me using a donor egg." Shannon at this point wasn't even thirty-five yet, so it wasn't that her eggs were too old. They just weren't implanting and blooming inside of her and growing. She continued, "And Dr. Paulson said, 'If you use one of Heather's eggs, since you are sisters, the baby will be twenty-five percent your own DNA.' What do you think?"

My sister Shannon. Just two hot moms on a private jet to Las Vegas, where I opened for Chelsea at Casears Palace.

Now, Shannon and I had shared clothes. We even had shared bikini bottoms once, which should be illegal even between sisters, but my bikini bottom was wet and there is nothing more uncomfortable than putting on a wet bathing suit. Even though we had shared so much already, I had never even considered the possibility of us sharing eggs.

Before I was married, I'd spent a weekend in Newport Beach, a very wealthy beach community in Southern California. I was having my coffee at the local Starbucks while perusing *South Coast* magazine and the *Orange County Register,* and I had never seen so many advertisements looking for young women to donate their eggs. Some were willing to pay up to twenty grand for the right egg. All the ads were asking for women in perfect health whose family had also had a history of good health. I had that. My grandmother on my dad's side had lived well into her nineties. When she died at ninety-one, it was discovered she was actually ninety-nine but changed her age at Ellis Island. How great is that? I would spend three weeks on a smelly, cramped ship if it meant I could scrape eight years of my age without anyone knowing. They also all asked for women who were over five-foot-nine, which I am. In fact, I'm five-foot-nine and a half, which I thought gave me an added bonus. Some ads were for blondes, but plenty asked for brunettes; all had to be college graduates and under thirty years old with good SAT scores. I had all these attributes, and for a moment as I looked out at Newport Harbor, I imagined being twenty thousand dollars richer and giving my egg to some super-wealthy childless couple. At the time I was auditioning a lot and was rarely ever getting a callback. I thought how nice it would feel for someone to finally choose me and say yes, you're the one, even if it wasn't a part in a TV show. It would still be very flattering. But then I started getting a little jealous of my egg and the life it would have growing up right by the water. My egg would probably have its own yacht and a big gorgeous house decorated in anchors. I actually called a clinic and asked whether you actually had to show your SAT scores. When they said yes, I knew I most likely wouldn't be picked. Don't get me wrong, my SAT scores were decent, but it was my essay on Ronald Reagan's influence on the sitcom *Family Ties* that got me accepted into the seven universities to which I applied. I decided that my egg would probably grow up to be a spoiled brat living in Newport Beach and if she ended up going to USC, she'd be a Delta Gamma, because all the girls from Newport who go to USC become Delta Gammas. I was a Gamma Phi, so I couldn't have that on my conscience. But when my own sister was considering my egg, it was totally different. I knew the kind of parents Shannon and Michael would be to my egg, and I knew it wouldn't grow up to be spoiled, or ungrateful, and if it did become a Delta Gamma, it wouldn't be because of the town it was raised in. Besides, Shannon was only asking for my egg, not for me to carry it for nine months, which I think is a much bigger favor to ask.

Can you imagine if you carried someone's baby for them and then they refused to do a favor for you when you asked? It would be hard not to be a little passive-aggressive and say, "No, I don't want to put you out by having you pick me up from the airport. I know you're busy with your child—the child that was only possible because of me, which I'm reminded of every time I look in the mirror and see the purple stretch marks across my abdomen. No, I don't mind never wearing a bikini again; besides one-piece bathing suits are back in. It was a sacrifice I was happy to make so you could celebrate Mother's Day while I wait at the airport for a cab." Donating an egg would just require a few hours in the doctor's office. (Unlike George Lopez's wife, who gave him one of her kidneys, only for George to divorce her a few short years later.) I told Shannon I was flattered that she wanted my egg and that I'd have to think about it.

For the next couple of days I couldn't think about anything else. Was Shannon even sure she wanted my egg? Drake was healthy, though I have to be honest, here, Drake was slow to roll. Babies are typically supposed to be able to roll over from their backs onto their tummies by themselves at around four to five months. At five and a half months Drake hadn't done it yet, and I was getting concerned. I expressed this concern to my friend Tara, and she told me not to worry, but what does she know? She wasn't a mother. The next day Tara's and my mutual friend, Nicole, called me out of the blue. Nicole's son was born a few weeks after Drake. We did some small talk and then she started talking about her son, Dylan. She said, "Dylan is just rolling and rolling all around my apartment. I can barely keep up with him. He sees a toy that he wants and he just rolls until he gets it. Good thing we don't live on a hill." Well, that doesn't even make sense. If you lived on a hill, would you put the baby on the grass and let him just roll down it? I tried to change the subject and talk about how cute Drake is when he just lays there flailing his limbs like a turtle on his back, and how he's so flexible he can suck on his own big toe. But Nicole would interrupt and say, "Dylan used to suck on his big toe about a month ago but now that he can roll, he is just into so many more sophisticated things than his toes."

I reminded Shannon that Drake still hadn't rolled over on his own yet, and asked her if that worried her. She just laughed and said, "Heather, I know your egg would be amazing but I also know it's weird."

I talked to my dad about giving my egg to Shannon. I thought he'd be all for it, since he used to hide the Easter eggs for Shannon and me. He went to great lengths to ensure that we both ended up with twelve each. I already had a baby, so wouldn't he want Shannon to have a baby too to keep it fair? But my dad, the former combat Marine said, "This is like when you girls would swap Halloween candy. This isn't about sharing a goddamn Snickers bar." He began to raise his voice. "It's one thing to share your K-ration of SPAM with a fellow Marine in a foxhole, but sharing eggs, what the hell is this? An omelet? This sounds like some hippie-dippy shit to me, and it's gonna backfire, baby, like an AK-47." I tried to explain how by having my egg Shannon would be raising a baby with part of her own DNA. My dad cut me off and said, "I know all about DNA. I watched the O.J. Simpson trial from start to finish. You don't want those O.J. detectives on it. I just think it will cause problems. You're opening up a whole can of worms, baby."

"Or in this case, a carton of eggs," I joked. However, I did see my dad's point. What if Shannon got my one winner egg and I was left with the loser eggs? It can happen. I've seen it

Me as the Octo-
mom—aka "The
woman with one too
many eggs."

in my own family. Out of the five kids all born to the same
mother and father, only Shannon and I went to college, and
my parents faced many challenges raising the other three.
That is one of the reasons Shannon became a criminal defense attorney, so she could help out my siblings, which she
has done pro bono over and over again. This is especially true
for my brother Rob, who was arrested for stalking. Don't get
freaked out, it was really a misunderstanding. He was working security at a Home Depot and someone in Kitchen Appli-
ances said hi, and he got the wrong impression. He was the
world's worst stalker, leaving answering-machine messages
with his phone number and mailing love letters with his return address, so Shannon had to defend him. When she'd visit
him in jail, he'd tell her that some of the other inmates would

say, "Oh man, how'd you get such a hot attorney? That's who I want representing me, homie."

My mom always tried to make the best of the situation and said to me, "We're all going to watch your sister defend your brother at the courthouse today." When I'd object and say it was depressing, she'd argue, "Come on, what kind of sister are you? They always come out to see your stand-up. Besides, it's Margarita Monday and I've got a coupon for Acapulco's, so we can all go there after, it will be fun!"

At the hearing, my mom would whisper to me, "Doesn't Shannon look stunning in that red suit, and who knew orange was Rob's color?" What if that happened to us? What if I gave away my Shannon egg and was only left with the Rob egg? I imagined twenty-five years into the future, me sitting at Shannon's son's medical-school graduation, and when they announced his name, "Whatever Goldstein," I'd be compelled to lean over to the stranger sitting to my right and say, "You know, he's not only my nephew. He's actually my son." Then I would lean over to my left and roll my giant son, Drake, over from his tummy to his back so he could see the rest of the scholars graduate.

I told Shannon Dad's reaction and his concerns about me giving her my egg and she said, "Well, I've seen the donors in Dr. Paulson's office waiting room. Once there was a girl around thirty and she had come down from San Jose with her sister and they seemed happy; they were making a weekend out of it."

"Well, what did the woman look like?" I asked.

"She was fine-looking, with blond hair," Shannon said.

"How thick was it?" I asked.

"How thick was what?" she questioned.

"Her hair. Was it thick and shiny, or flat and dull?" I asked.

"I don't remember," she answered.

"Well, I don't think you should pick an egg from someone who doesn't have good hair. You and I both have really good hair. Do you want your daughter to have to suffer through hours of having painful and expensive hair extensions sewn into her scalp? How much would an egg from a woman like that cost anyway?" I asked.

"I think they pay them a standard fee of, like, three thousand dollars," she answered.

"Three thousand dollars, that's it? That's not what they were offering in Newport Beach for eggs," I said.

"Well, I guess that is because this is not a Newport Beach egg. It's a San Jose egg." Shannon laughed. "Heather, don't worry about it. If we even do it at all it's not going to be for a few months. Michael just wants to enjoy the Jacuzzi again without stressing that it's killing his sperm count."

I thought about the show *Big Love* on HBO, where one man has three wives. They have their own babies but they all share the same husband and help raise each other's children. Not that my sister and I would do that, because she lives a few hours away, but they seemed pretty happy. Even today sometimes I really feel like I could use a sister wife, not so she could have sex with Peter on Tuesdays and Thursdays, but just to help out with the homework and the school projects. I'm not crafty, and those Mormons really know their way around a glue gun. On TLC's *Sister Wives,* when the sole husband,

Kory, was going to get a fourth wife, at first the other three wives seemed happy. I think because they thought she'd help babysit their thirteen kids. But that all changed when wife number four was instantly pregnant. Now that I'm thinking about it, I don't want a sister wife.

I would like to be on a reality show called *Gusbands*. It's me and my three gay husbands and what we go through all living under one roof. Each gay husband I choose would have a quality that I need in a partner. One would help dress me and curl the back of my hair; another would be really good at computers and paying our bills, like my current real husband; and one would be an amazing chef and an interior decorator. The gusbands would have conflict with one another (because that is what makes for great reality TV) and they'd get all pissy with one another just like they do on *Sister Wives*. I'd have special nights designated with each one but then during awards season I'd inevitably spend more time with the stylist one, and that would just be something the other two would have to accept if we were going to make this family work. And there are no kids. The three gay husbands just cater to me and vie for my attention.

But Shannon didn't want three gay husbands, she wanted one baby. So one night I called her and I said, "I know I'm not the smartest woman in the world, but I also know I don't have a learning disability. And even though I'm not athletic, and have a tendency to trip on my own feet a lot, I am in excellent health. Besides, I'm tall and have great full, thick, shiny hair and have some unique talents for impersonating people and telling crass jokes. My point is, I'm not perfect but I'm better than some San Jose egg, and if you decide you want my eggs you can have some of them." Shannon began to cry, as did I, and she said it meant a lot to her that I was willing to share whatever piece of an omelet I had.

Shannon still had four frozen embryos, so she decided to implant those before using an egg donor and, lo and behold, one of them took. Shannon gave birth to her son, not conceived on a rock but in a lab where it had waited six months to be defrosted and then cooked to perfection. When Michael held his son for the first time, he said to the nurse, "Have you ever heard of 50 Cent? Well, meet 75 Grand." Yes, in-vitro is very expensive but worth every penny. Three years later, Shannon hadn't had her period in a couple of months and wanted to drink alcohol so she sent Michael out to get a pregnancy test. Sure enough, it was positive. At thirty-nine, Shannon gave birth to a daughter who was conceived the old-fashioned and cheaper way.

I have a single friend who went to Dr. Paulson a few years ago to freeze her eggs so that later on, if she met the right guy, she could say, "Yes I'm forty-two, but I've got eggs that are only thirty-eight waiting to meet your sperm whenever you are ready to start a family with me." Now, I hope that is not the first sentence that comes out of her mouth on a first date, but essentially that is the thought behind freezing them. She is very successful and could afford the procedure and saw it as insurance. A few of us met for dinner after she had frozen the eggs and she said, "Dr. Paulson said he had never seen such good-looking eggs before. He was able to get eleven eggs from me, which I guess is unheard of. He said the cells were just so full and perfectly round." I mean, was she serious? This is the same woman who rolls her eyes when I talk about my kids, and I don't even brag.

In fact, I do the opposite of bragging. When someone compliments Drake on his baseball techniques, I say, "Well, he's been on five teams already. He started really young and he works privately with a coach just to strengthen his pitch. He actually should be doing better." But bragging about an egg that hasn't even met sperm in a Petri dish yet is just too much. I feel like saying, "Well, Cindy, you can relate, being that you're a mother to eleven brilliant eggs. I don't know how you do it all? It must be that great day care you send them to, La Freezer. I wish my kids weren't so spazzy in a restaurant. Yours are so still they haven't moved for years."

One thing I'd like to do is to clone myself and raise a mini-me as my daughter. The way I understand it is that the baby would be exactly like me. It would look like me, and have my personality and everything. I would love to tell her when she is fourteen, "Don't worry, your head will shrink in a few years and you won't look like you have Lupus anymore." I'd also like to tell her, "No matter how many miles you ride your bike up a hill, your ankles will never get bigger in circumference. Your calves are always going to resemble those of a baby colt that has just been birthed." We'd have such a good time together because I'd know everything she likes, but eventually she'd get to the stage where she wouldn't shut the fuck up and I'd have to ask her to move out and pursue blue-balling guys until she found one she liked who would marry her and put up with her crap.

22

I DON'T WANT TO BORE YOU WITH THESE STORIES, BUT . . .

Have you ever noticed how kidnap victim and bestselling author Jaycee Dugard has amazing skin? Sometimes I think about things like that. She's now in her early thirties, and she still looks fifteen. It's imperative to avoid the outside, pretty much forever. So when I went to my son's soccer game recently, I was frustrated that we could not find which field our team was playing on. I was dragging two heavy chairs, a whiny kid, and one soccer ball at a large university that had twenty-six fields with fifty-two different uniforms all merging into one. My son's uniform is orange with a hint of black on the sleeve. We would spot an orange team, and I would make him go play with the little orange men until Brandon discovered that this particular team had a hint of *navy* on their uniform's shirt. We trudged on to another soccer field with orange uniforms only to get closer to see that they were girls and not his team either. I was fighting back tears, saying to myself, Life is too short, who cares about soccer? This is America, not Argentina. By the time we found the correct field, I felt I had experienced the agony of defeat and the thrill of victory.

I immediately placed my folding chair in the one space available underneath the shade. Then Brandon came up to me and said, "You're not on my team's side; you're on the Dyno Blasters' side."

I said, "But that side is blazing hot. Don't you remember when you and Mommy watched the TV special about the girl who was kidnapped and didn't go out in the sun for eighteen years? Do you remember how she didn't have a hint of crow's feet underneath her eyes? I'm sorry, Brandon, but I'm going to cheer for you in the shade. Complexion is more important than competition."

Brandon started to get upset and I was all weary from the long walk, so I agreed to sit in the blazing-hot sun and slathered on some sunscreen. There's just something about the smell of Coppertone as it seeps into my baking skin that just makes me really crave a margarita.

My father sat down next to me and he soon started telling me the stories I had heard my whole life, including how his first job was selling Schick razors to pharmacies, and how he headed up the Coca-Cola account for his advertising firm, and of course the inevitable Marine stories. Maybe because I was no longer a teenager or being overly distracted as a busy mom, I actually started to listen to his stories with interest. He told me how it was to be a young boy in Long Beach, New York. "Well, my best friend, Monty McKinney, and I, used to go into the caves by the beach and smoke cigarettes that we stole from our parents. One day when we were there, we saw two of our other friends' older brothers, who were about fifteen, fucking each other in the ass. . . . Oh, I don't want to bore you with these stories. Do you want to hear a story about when I was working on the Toyota account?"

The game had ended and my father was in the middle of this juicy story.

I said, "Wait, Dad, so the two teenage boys were gay?"

He replied, "Well, no, I don't think so. I think they were experimenting."

I said, "Did they know that you even saw them?"

He replied, "No, and Monty and I never talked about it again."

I said, "Dad, no, I think they were gay."

My father said, "But they both went on to get married. One had eight kids, and the other had eleven."

I said, "Dad, this sounds like a version of *Brokeback Mountain,* where they were in love but had secret rendezvous in Long Beach until one of them died."

My father said, "Now, *Brokedown Hill,* wasn't that with the Heath Bar Ledger who took too many pills and died, and then his wife became Marilyn Monroe?"

I said, "Dad, you've screwed up movies with actors' real lives, but that's not the point. What you're missing here is eternal love that wasn't accepted."

He said, "Well, Heather, maybe you're on to something."

I said, "Dad you have been telling me some boring stories over time. Why do you pick today to tell me a real juicy one?"

He replied, "I don't know. It just popped up in my memory. I am eighty-five. I've got plenty of other juicy stories, but none of the other ones involve me walking in on two men fucking, so I don't know if you'd be interested."

"You're right, Dad, I wouldn't."

My parents are settling into their golden years. Whenever my friends see them together, they say, "It's so cute. Your parents are so in love."

I reply, "Yeah, they really are in love now, but they sure didn't come across that way in 1988 when I was a teenager and would go to bed dreaming about how I wished one of them would have the sense to call a good divorce attorney."

I think this goes to show that kids sometimes do factor into a divorce. People always tell their children, "Mommy and Daddy are getting a divorce, but it has nothing to do with you." But I call bullshit on that. Eighty-five percent of my fights with Peter are over the kids. If they weren't around, we would only have 15 percent the number of fights. Just yesterday, I gave Brandon some milk in a cup and he accidently spilled it. Peter then started criticizing the cup I chose. I argued back that if he felt that strongly about it, he could have gotten off his ass and poured him the milk in the first place. See, my point is, if Brandon didn't exist, that fight would have never taken place.

It seems the divorced woman is almost celebrated now. It's like, "You go, girl. You kicked that guy to the curb. You were so brave to leave. Sisters are doing it for themselves."

How come no women stand around saying, "You know, I have so much respect for Jackie. She's been married to that obese fat fuck of an asshole and she just continues to wake up with a smile on her face year after year. What a strong woman she is."?

I wonder why it is that no one is celebrating the woman who stays and gets through the shitty teenage years with their kids. So then when a couple is alone again, there's the possibility of them rekindling their love, just like my parents did.

23

MY HIATUS

I had two weeks off from *Chelsea Lately,* a break we call a hiatus. Most of my colleagues went on exotic vacations or booked stand-up gigs. I, however, decided to spend my days off being the perfect mother and wife, volunteering at my children's school and attending a *Playboy* charity golf tournament with my husband. In short, I was planning to win the Mother and Wife of the Year Award.

On my first day off, I walked Brandon to his kindergarten class, like many mothers do. As I walked back from his class, my neighbor snarkily called out to me, "You're actually here on campus. We never see you." Through clenched teeth, I said back, "Yeah, I am." As if a mother would ever say that to a working father whom she happened to spot at school. It doesn't help that everyone at the school thinks Peter is so wonderful. He happens to be the only father at St. Ignatius who is invited to the Mothers' Appreciation Luncheon, where he enjoys sipping white wine and nibbling on tiny cucumber tea sandwiches while the ladies toast him for putting together his very successful golf tournament. I mean, sure, Peter did raise money for the school, but let's be honest—Peter being the chairman of a golf tournament is like me offering to wear free Gucci clothes to help get the word out about Gucci's green initiatives. It's a little self-serving. He's certainly not Mother Teresa reincarnated.

Peter enjoying his tea while being honored at the ladies' luncheon.

Later in the week I was asked if I could volunteer at St. Ignatius's annual Easter-egg hunt. I immediately offered my help. The e-mail included a list of what to bring. Upon close consideration, I decided a bag of mini bagels was a lot easier than cut-up fruit or homemade cupcakes. In fact, since I was feeling especially generous, I wrote back to the room mom that I would bring not one, but *two* dozen bagels, so no one else had to purchase any. I have to admit, it felt pretty good. I was definitely on my way to making up for missing the robot parade (in which Brandon's was hands-down the worst one). However, the night before the big hunt another e-mail was sent to me stating, "Please make sure the bagels you bring are made with no peanuts, to protect the children who are allergic."

"Oh shit," I said as I read my iPhone. How is it that I always pick the wrong thing? I thought bagels would be easier than carving strawberries into the shape of red rosebuds, and honestly mini bagels are the entrée of the kindergarten Easter brunch. After inspecting the back of the bagel package, I was relieved to read that there were no peanuts used in the making of the mini bagels. Phew. Super Mom prevails for once in her life.

The next morning I carefully chose my outfit. The previous day I had volunteered for library duty and made the crucial mistake of wearing a skirt with a hem that met with most of the kindergartners' heads. I chose sensible, loose-fitting tan slacks with a button-down, long-sleeve shirt and flats. I looked like I was straight off the pages of the Ellen DeGeneres ad in the JCPenney catalog. I grabbed my twenty-four peanut-free bagels and arrived in the school's play yard a whole eight minutes early to help set up. How do I do it? I thought as I imaginarily patted myself on my conservatively clothed back. I cut each bagel in half and placed them on tiny bunny plates around the luncheon tables. With a few minutes to spare before the children came, the other mothers and I began to talk about our plans for Easter Sunday. Then one mother, Tammy, asked, "Who brought the bagels?"

"I did. I brought all twenty-four."

"Did you check the ingredients for peanuts?" she asked.

"Yes, I did—no peanuts," I said proudly.

"Where were the bagels made?" she questioned.

I balked. "I don't know. I bought them at Ralphs," I said.

Tammy just stared at me with her eyes widening, so I continued: "I got them in the bakery section, next to the hot dog buns."

"Well, we need to know if the bagels were made in the vicinity of a peanut factory," Tammy said seriously. "We have two airbornes." Airbornes, what did that mean?

She continued, "Two of the children are so allergic to peanuts that they can't even be near a product that was made in the proximity of peanuts. They could be affected because the peanut particles are airborne."

Oh my God. My heart started beating faster. "I don't know if they were made near a peanut factory," I said.

"Well, where is the package that they came in?" said another mother, trying to be helpful.

"I threw it away," I said.

"Which trash can? We'll look," she replied.

"No, I threw it away at home this morning so I could bring them in a cute wicker basket so I'd look more like a homemade mother."

I instantly imagined one of the airbornes holding their little throats and being placed in a helicopter to be airlifted to a children's hospital and everyone knowing it was me who brought the bagels. So I took my cute basket and with less than sixty seconds to spare picked up all twenty-four bagels off the bunny plates and dumped them in the large trash can in the kitchen. Then, of course, I started to cry. I said, "I'm sorry, you guys. I know how hard it is to be a room mom and I ruined the one thing I wanted to help with." As they began to console me, the kids came barreling out of their class, grabbing plastic eggs with hidden candy in them. I wiped my tears and hugged Brandon as he showed me his starburst eggs. Then I thought, Who wants a bagel when you have candy? I now always sign up first so I can bring the paper goods—I found an amazing brand that is 100 percent nut-free.

The following day was Friday. I was off to volunteer in Drake's class to help with their painting projects, which the parents would bid on at an auction. Each student paints his or her name and a small picture on either a serving platter or a tile to all be put together on a bench or a patio table. It goes for hundreds or sometimes thousands of dollars, depending on how much the parents care about possessing the ultimate childhood memory.

Every year I donate a basket full of Chelsea Handler–signed books, *Chelsea Lately* T-shirts, and Chuy bobbleheads. After I dropped off the kids at school, I parked the car and walked the basket in so everyone could see me with it. It was pretty heavy and included four VIP tickets to a taping, so I figured it would go for at least a couple hundred dollars. Just then I saw Sheila Baker. From across the parking lot, she yelled, "Wow, twice in one week, what's going on? Is Peter out of town?"

"No, I'm dropping off my very large donation for the auction. Books and tickets to the show I work on every day to provide milk, bread, and Nestlé Toll House Chocolate-Chip Cookies for my family of five," I said, very matter-of-factly.

"Oh, I'll take it for you. I'm sure you have to get into hair and makeup, right?" she said as she grabbed both sides of the basket.

Ouch. I had actually put on makeup that day and even brushed my hair, but I'd be damned if I let her drop it off and not get full credit. Just then I looked down into the basket and noticed something pink, almost fleshy-colored, peeking between the *Chelsea Chelsea Bang Bang* book and a "Homo You Didn't" shirt. (It's a very pro-gay T-shirt, which happens to be our top seller.) What is that? I thought. Then it hit me. It was a rubber vagina that a sex company had sent to the *Chelsea Lately* offices. I must have left the basket alone in my office for a second.

"Heather, let me take it. I'm in charge of writing the descriptions of all the silent auction items," Sheila said nicely.

Oh my God she could not take this. How would she describe what she found: "A Night of Laughter: four VIP tickets to a taping of E!'s number-one show, *Chelsea Lately*; five *NY Times* bestselling books, all signed by the author, valued at eighty dollars; and one anatomically correct vagina—priceless." I pulled the basket close to my chest and said, "Sorry, I just remembered I have one more thing in my car I need to add to it." I turned on my heel and headed back. I still don't know for sure who put that vagina in my Catholic-school silent-auction basket, but I would bet it was Josh Wolf or Chris Franjola or Sarah Colonna or Jen Kirkman or Fortune Feimster, or even the grand master herself—Chelsea.

Having not scored a perfect 10 at the boys' school, I felt I could at least be the world's best wife by taking Peter to the annual *Playboy* golf tournament. The first thing I had to do was buy a super-cute golf outfit, since I never play unless it's miniature with the boys.

When I got to Golf Smith, a tony boutique, my eyes were immediately drawn to a hot-pink gingham skirt. I first tried on a small and I couldn't even get it over my thighs. Then I tried a medium and it was still too small. What was going on? Are golf clothes all made for Asian women, or what? Finally, the large fit me. When I was grabbing a pink visor, I mentioned to the salesgirl how much I loved my outfit but that it ran so small, and she said, "Well, it's juniors."

"Like, for middle-schoolers?" I asked.

Me in my golf outfit from the juniors department.

"Yes," she answered. I was a little humiliated but mostly relieved that I wasn't actually a large. I was going to be competing with scantily clad Playmates. How else could I compete unless I was dressed like a twelve-year-old?

Once we arrived at the tournament, I was pleased to be greeted by a Bloody Mary. Maybe real golf is more fun than I thought. The celebrities were few and far between, to be honest, which explains why I was invited. There were also some professional football players there. I didn't recognize any because I don't follow sports unless the players are ten years of age and under. One guy from the San Francisco Giants did stop me to say how much he and his girlfriend enjoyed reading my book while on the beach in Hawaii. That made my day a home run, or rather a hole in one. Do you get it? If not, reread!

The girls working the event were about sixth-tier Playmates compared to the Playmates in the magazine—a little rough around the edges, with dark roots, some cellulite, maybe a missing tooth here or there, but still not a day over twenty-three, so the guys were happy. On the first hole we were greeted by four of the girls, dressed in their little Playboy golf outfits. Mine was definitely cuter and possibly skimpier. It was a good day out with Peter and I know I definitely scored a lot of relationship points. I must admit, our relationship is not perfect.

I think the biggest problem plaguing my marriage right now is Peter's snoring. He doesn't just snore. He has sleep apnea. I know this for a fact because I don't mean to brag but we have medical insurance and I sent him to the university to spend the night and he was professionally diagnosed. This means that he actually stops breathing in between snorts. They gave him this sleeping apparatus that he is supposed to wear over his nose and mouth that looks like something out of the movie *Alien,* but he didn't like it, so he was like screw this thing, I'll just smoke a cigar and have another bottle of wine and just continue to snore. Some nights are so bad and the pauses between snores are so long that I actually think he is dead and start planning his funeral. I'd choose a simple black wrap dress and I would go with wedge heels because it will be easier when walking on the grass at Forest Lawn Cemetery. I'm going with pre-made deli sandwiches. I don't care what my mother says; I think it is weird to force people to make their own sandwiches, especially when they are in mourning. No one likes that yellow bread, and you have so much Russian dressing left over. At this point, he'll usually snort so loud it will break me out of styling his funeral and back into reality and I'll pop up out of bed and ask, "Did you cross over to the other side? Did you see Papa Joe? Did you talk to Amy Winehouse? Is she still mad at me for impersonating her?"

On our recent trip to San Francisco for a gig at a comedy club, his snoring became unbearable. Every time he'd get a little bit quiet I'd think, Heather, fall asleep, fall asleep, fall asleep, then: SNORE. It was so frustrating that I got up and went to the front desk of the hotel and got another room for the night. A very empathetic, extremely well-dressed gay man on duty listened to me rant about why I had to get my own room and how we were happily married but I just really needed my sleep. I was going to go straight to the room but then I thought Peter might wake up and think I was kidnapped. So I went back to the room to leave a note saying "Hey fat fuck, Your snoring was so out of control that I got another room. I did 6 shows this weekend so I can afford it." When I opened the door to our room, it was silent. His snoring had completely stopped. Fuck, my dramatics were unnecessary and cost me $219. I still left the note and went to the room in the hopes that he'd feel a little guilty when he woke up. Unfortunately, I woke up and returned to the room before he even opened his eyes. He'd had the best sleep of his life and had no idea what I had been through.

So maybe my hiatus didn't work out as planned. Maybe I'll never be the perfect wife and mother. But at least I have a job that allows me to afford cute golf outfits from the juniors department and a separate hotel room from my husband.

24

RED-CARPET READY

I'm not the best disciplinarian. I often say no to things that my kids ask for but then give in and say yes after the ninth "But Mom." I joke with them, but I really hate being called "But Mom." My name is Mom and I have a butt. However, I do not like being called "Butt Mom." It's a horrible name to call your mother. Sometimes I even sign my letters "Love, Butt Mom." Because I feel that is the name I most often hear.

There was one incident that took place a couple of weeks ago in our home. Drake was acting up and all I had to say was, "Do you remember the broken-cookie incident?" His eyes widened and he experienced the horrible flashback known as the "broken cookie" like a soldier who goes through post-traumatic stress.

In our house we have what we call a cookie party. We buy those Nestlé's Toll House cookie packages with the cookie dough already made into itsy-bitsy squares. We then put them on a cookie sheet and into the oven and ta-da! It's a cookie party. One night, my husband started the cookie party at eight thirty on a school night. I thought this was a little late for a cookie party, but I didn't try to stop it because, well, I'm a cool mom. When the cookies came out, Peter said to Drake, "Now, don't use the spatula to scoop the cookie off the pan until they've cooled, otherwise the cookies will break apart." I was not aware that this conversation had taken place, and about two minutes after I entered the kitchen, I saw the cookie pan, got a spatula, and began to scoop one cookie up as Drake witnessed it breaking apart. He immediately started to whine and say, "Mom, you broke the cookie! You broke the cookie! You didn't let it cool first! You ruined it!" I tried to calm him down and said, "Drake, it's fine. It still tastes good." He continued and began flailing his arms around. "No, Mom, you ruined it. Dad said not to take them off the pan yet, and you did and now the cookie is broken."

Much like the critically acclaimed Oxygen show *Snapped,* a true-crime series about women who have committed murder, or attempted murder, where often the target is the individual's spouse, the thing that ties all the stories together is that something caused a normal woman to finally just snap and go into a murderous rage. That is what happened to me that night, except fortunately the only thing I ended up murdering was the freshly baked Nestlé's Toll House cookies. I snapped. Looking at my whining, ungrateful son, I turned to him as my voice lowered like Linda Blair possessed by the devil in the movie *The Exorcist* and I said, "You will not cry over a broken cookie when there are millions of children in

Haiti who don't even have clean water to drink. Sean Penn has to divide the water up! You ungrateful little shit! Now no one gets cookies!"

Poor Brandon was just sitting there and not complaining at all and would have devoured a broken cookie even if it fell on the dirty garage floor. It was too late. I took the cookie sheet and dumped all the cookies in the trash can. I said, "Drake ruined it for both of you." Drake continued to whine and cry and tried to explain that he was justified in being upset that I broke the cookie, so I ordered him to his room.

I went back out to the kitchen and was trying to calm myself down when Peter said, "Well, you know you shouldn't have tried to take the cookies off the pan until they were fully cooled." I turned to him in horror and yelled, "What, you think Drake's reaction is justified over a broken cookie? What kind of monsters are we raising?"

After a few minutes Drake was still crying, which pissed me off even more that he was being so dramatic, so I opened his door and stomped into his room and picked up a giant LEGO helicopter Drake had just spent three hours putting together and I said, "You want to cry about a broken cookie? What about a broken LEGO helicopter? I'll take every LEGO in here and give them to little boys who don't know the difference between LEGOs and the LEGO knockoff, Eurobricks. Do you know how many times I've stepped on one of your LEGOs and suffered? I have the scar on my heel to prove it. It is a rectangle with two small circles in it!"

Drake kept crying and said, "But Mom, you're bullying me." I don't know what angered me more, being called "Butt Mom" for the hundredth time or being accused of being a bully.

I said to him, "Bullying? A parent can't bully their child. You will not use the buzzword of 2012 on me, mister! I'm so sick of bullying. I'm being bullied by people talking about bullying. I'm trying to teach you to be grateful for what you have." At that point, I looked up and saw my reflection in Drake's mirrored closet doors and what I saw was terrifying. I was becoming Betty Broderick, whom Meredith Baxter won an Emmy for portraying in my all-time favorite made-for-TV movie.

Before the cookie party was supposed to start, I was in the middle of trying on nine potential dresses for a red-carpet event the following night. It was for the Gracie Awards, which honors women in television. The other female writers on the *Chelsea Lately* staff and I were going to accept an award on Chelsea's behalf. I had been sent cocktail dresses on loan to choose from, but each one I tried on was not working. They were all too tight, too short, and too booby. I had come out to have Peter zip one dress that I thought would work and as I took a deep breath and sucked it all in, he took one look at me and said, "No, I'm not going to even bother. You look like a New Jersey housewife." I ripped off the Garden State dress and tried on another brightly hued satin minidress. I was getting so frustrated, because I wanted to look like a classy lady writer, not a cougar in heat. To help get the dresses zipped up I had put on my industrial-strength Spanx, which is like an entire one-piece bodysuit that goes up over my bra and all the way down into shorts to mid-thigh. It is so tight, I have to jump up and down to get it on to the point where I work up a pretty decent sweat. Drake then said again, "Butt Mom, you're bullying me!" Then I screamed again, "A mother can't bully her son. What is that private school I'm paying for teaching you?" Just then I looked up into Drake's mirror and saw an evil woman in a binding, nude-colored contraption wearing nothing else but a pair of red pumps and her hair in a severe bun screaming back at me. I realized at that moment that I was more frightening than Joan Crawford with Noxzema smeared on her face screaming at her adopted daughter, Christina, about wire hangers. I'm not proud of this moment, but I'm honest about it. I put the LEGO helicopter down next to the LEGO airplane and the LEGO airport and walked into my bedroom and peeled off the Spanx straightjacket and put on my flannel pajamas. I returned to Drake's room and gave him a glass of water and a big hug and kiss and told him I loved him. Then I went to Brandon's room. He was already asleep and I kissed his sweet cheek.

I chose to tell this story in my book because this way Drake is less likely to write about it in his book thirty years

Wearing my own dress in the bathroom of the Beverly Hills Hotel before accepting the Gracie Award with other pretty, funny women Jen Kirkman and Sarah Colonna.

from now or write a movie about his barely famous mother from which this will be the scene that gay men reenact at fabulous dinner parties for years to come.

The following night was the Gracie Awards, and I had decided on a long dress I had bought myself a year and a half earlier. I will never forget how much fun we had that night, and Drake never will forget the story of the broken cookie. We still have cookie parties regularly, mostly without Butt Mom. I have yet to make chocolate-chip cookie dough from scratch, but now I always make sure they cool and Drake never complains about what they look like. Even if they are burnt, he is well aware that there are children who have had nothing in their lives but burnt cookies, with no water, and are thrilled to eat them.

EPILOGUE

Here are a few stories that didn't make the final cut, but I still think they are funny.

For me the kids playing organized sports is still no picnic. But recently I found a silver lining when we were at the first soccer game of the season and the team mom asked loudly, "Who was on team snack today? Hello, the kids are starving. Oh, let me check, Dobias, Dobias?" What is great is that my husband and my kids have the last name of Dobias, but I'm Heather McDonald, so I confidently replied, "I'm McDonald, I don't know who Dobias is. See you next Saturday."

I admit I pick up the kids' food if it falls on the gravel and give it back to them, but only if I'm positive no other parent can see me. I also admit that if it weren't for the Skittles I smuggled into the batting cage, my boys would never hit the ball. Am I worried that Skittles are a gateway drug to steroids? Yes, but then again if my boys ever get to the point that they're considering taking steroids because they are that passionate about a sport, I'd be impressed, because I've never been very athletic.

If my boys get hurt on the field I've been strictly instructed to stay back and not come to their aid, because in Drake's words "Your face makes me cry." At first I didn't know how to take it, but then like most things I just decided to take it as a compliment. I also do this when it comes to comments made to me on Twitter. On Twitter, unlike Facebook, you can write to anybody; you don't have to be their friend. My Twitter name is cleverly titled @HeatherMcDonald and I'd love to hear from you. Most people write nice and funny things to me and I really enjoy it, but there was this one person named @FionaJewSilverstein who would write to me every day saying things like "You're not funny. Why does @ChelseaHandler let you on her show." Or "You're so ugly. You look like the puppet Billy in the Saw movies." Well I'm not into horror movies so I Googled "Puppet Billy in Saw" and you know what, I kind of look like it. I can't lie. But at least I resemble someone who was a lead in a major motion picture with several successful sequels. And then I decided to finally respond to her and I wrote "Dear @FionaJewSilverstein I'm sorry you don't like my comedy or my face but I will continue to pray that Jesus allows you into heaven."

I recently went to a benefit silent auction at St. Ignatius on a mission to corner one of the nuns who was also active at my old all-girls high school that I wanted Mackenzie to also attend. Mackenzie had gotten a bad grade in science because of not putting in enough work on her seventh-grade science project, but I knew she could do the work if she tried and was more open with Peter and me.

I was able to talk to Sister Therese, whom I knew from my time at the school, and she made me feel better about getting Mackenzie in and told me to make sure on her application that it was clear she was my daughter. When I returned to the table I said to my friend Liz, "I knew she'd get a bad grade on that science project. It was so unoriginal, watering plants with three different kinds of water, *please*. What she should have done is taken tampons and soaked them in vodka and see how quickly the girls get drunk." Liz's pinot grigio shot through her nostrils. Wow, a captive audience at the St. Ignatius auction, I thought, I'm going to make up for last year. So I continued, "Not her friends, of course, I'm not that inappropriate, but I do know three girls at *Chelsea Lately*, four if you count Fortune, who would be willing to participate on any given Tuesday afternoon. How great would it be if you get different kinds of tampons and different types of vodka. You can chart the whole thing with graphs based on how long you let them soak versus the girl's height and weight. Then we could use Peter's Breathalyzer he bought off the Internet that he keeps at all times in his glove compartment just in case it is above .08 and we need to call a cab."

A good friend of mine recently asked me to perform at a comedy night to benefit his charity. I initially said no because

I know my act is not clean enough for most fifty-year-old Christians, and he is a fifty-year-old Christian. But he kept pressing me so Peter suggested I invite him and the event planner to my show so they could see the language and tone of my stand-up for themselves. They saw me perform, and convinced me to do their event. I began to get very excited about the charity. It's called "Mercy of the Valley," and it feeds and provides shelter for the Valley's homeless and their pets. I thought, what a perfect charity for me, it even has the word "Valley" in the title. Since it's also nondenominational, non-political, and basically nothing like a Catholic charity, I figured I wouldn't have to deal with the scandals that have rocked the church or its stance on gay marriage. I was simply feeding the homeless and their pets—who could argue with that?

We had a big meeting about the date, the theater, and all the press they were going to line up. I made it my introduction on *Chelsea Lately* so people would know where to buy tickets and told everyone about how great and non-discriminatory the charity was. The event was supposed to take place on November 2nd, and they decided to use the cover of this book to help promote the show. About six weeks before the big event, I was getting my morning coffee and starting to make the kids lunch when Peter said to me "The Mercy of the Valley event has been canceled." I turned quickly around "Why?" "Well they said since you are holding a big glass of Chardonnay on the cover of your book it is not appropriate for the image that the Mercy of the Valley homeless alcoholics want to be associated with." "What?" I yelled. "They're homeless in the Valley and I don't fit their image? That is amazing. Here, I chose them over the Catholic Church because I thought they'd be more inclusive. At least I know with certainty that I've never been to a Catholic event where there wasn't alcohol, including Mass itself! The only person they're discriminating against is me!" There is nothing like trying to go out of my way to help and then essentially being told that I'm not good enough. I now know what it must feel like to be a Republican politician who chooses a rock song for their campaign, only to get an angry call from the artist saying "Can you please stop playing my song at your rallies?"

When it comes to sex, after twelve years of marriage it is not the greatest form of foreplay to hear your husband say, "These condoms are about to expire so you want to do something about it?" The only thing that is more of a turnoff is when he knows I'm in the bedroom and he's in the bathroom sitting on the toilet with the *L.A. Times* and he grunts and says, "I can't do it. It's too big. It's crowning. I need an epidural, stat."

The other morning we were able to squeeze in sex before Brandon started pounding on the door yelling, "Open this door, lady." Peter let me relax in bed and got Brandon's Froot Loops, and as I laid there under the covers Mackenzie came in to ask me something and that's when she looked at my bare shoulders and then down to the floor where my pajamas were crumpled in a ball there. She arched her brow and asked, "And why aren't you wearing pajamas?" I never felt like such a dirty slut as I did in that moment. So of course I avoided eye contact with my twelve-year-old daughter and mumbled, "I got hot during the night."

We don't watch porn, but we do watch *Game of Thrones* and *Spartacus,* which is basically porn with a history lesson. The other night I was trying to go to sleep during an episode of *Spartacus* when I heard, "I'd like a whore on my cock." So I popped up and asked, "What year is this supposed to be happening?" Peter pulled out his iPad and quickly answered, "Seventy-five years before Christ. Don't you know that?"

"Well, you didn't know it. You just looked it up. Wow, if there was really this much fucking going on, this really makes Mary being a virgin even a bigger deal." As I continued watching, there was a scene with a naked woman in a bathtub with her one lady in waiting washing her back while her second lady in waiting was getting her off all while she was having a conversation with her husband. So I said to Peter, "This is so unreal. Look how huge that bathtub is. Do you know how long it would take to fill it with buckets of hot water from a well? By the time it was full it would be freezing and everyone's horniness would have cooled off. These girls look like they should be at a nightclub on Sunset Boulevard, not in Rome BC. At least they should grow out a full bush for authenticity."

How awful for these actresses to call home and say, "Hey, Mom and Dad, I got a guest role in a TV series. I play a maid who also has to bring her boss to orgasm in a bathtub while she and her husband plot her sister's death. I don't have a speaking role but I groan a lot."

I feel bad for girls like this, but not as bad as I still feel for Monica Lewinsky. I just really feel she was before her time. If a woman got caught giving Obama a blow job today she'd be revered by gold diggers of all ethnicities. She'd have a reality show and a nail-polish color specifically named after her. But since Monica became famous in the 1990s she barely got a handbag line off the ground. It's downright tragic.

Because Peter and I met before texting existed, we missed the whole sexting thing. I tried a few times to do it, but he didn't put much effort into writing back and I absolutely hate emoticons. I don't know why they piss me off but they do. It's just too cutesy to see a heart or a smiley face. So when I received a text from Peter starting off with a thumbs-up emoticon saying, "We have a foursome set for tomorrow morning," I immediately wrote him back saying, "This is your wife! What the hell is going on?" Luckily there was not a doubt in my mind that it was a foursome for golf and not a foursome of swingers. Peter wrote back, "Oops! That's funny. At least I didn't text 'Let's fuck at 9am.'" And he's right. I'd rather have him cheating on me with other heterosexual middle-aged golfers than women, even if the game takes several hours and for some reason no cell phone works on any golf course in all of North America, not Verizon, not AT&T, not T-Mobile, or at least that is what Peter tells me.

Peter is still cheap to the point that he tries to renegotiate the kids' library fines based on the book's current value on Amazon.com. I can't blame him; he is a mortgage broker. It is in his blood. So when he boasted that he got us front-row tickets at the circus, I was impressed, but then realized why the front-row seats were available, because no one else wants them based on the fact that you are just a few feet away from giant elephants dropping shit pounds at a time even as they dance and twirl about.

Peter once made us pretend we weren't a family because he had two coupons for a Mexican restaurant, but you're only supposed to use one coupon per family. I ordered with my daughter, Peter ordered with the boys, and then we sat at two different tables. Halfway through my burrito bowl Drake tried to talk to Mackenzie and she whispered in a panic, "No, Drake, we're not supposed to know each other. What Dad did was illegal, he could go to jail. We could lose the house, go away!"

The last couple of months I've been running into Adrienne Maloof from *The Real Housewives of Beverly Hills* at events around town and I really like her a lot. She has a nine-year-old son and six-year-old twin boys, exactly Drake's and Brandon's ages, and she sends them to a Catholic school just like ours but on the other side of town. Her husband met Peter and they talked golf. We planned on getting our families together and I couldn't have been more excited. I thought, This is the family I've been looking for all my life! To top it off she's a Real Housewife and he is a plastic surgeon! I couldn't wait to go swimming at her Beverly Hills mansion and be waited on by her staff while her husband injected me with Botox. We made tentative plans for a group family date, but a few days before we were supposed to meet up news broke on TMZ that she and her husband were getting divorced. I wrote Adrienne telling her I was sorry to hear what she was going through. I then went back on Craigslist to check whether any other families had responded to our ad.

ACKNOWLEDGMENTS

I'd like to thank my parents, Bob and Pam McDonald, for being the two best people in the world to have raised me. Thank you for always supporting and never doubting that I could accomplish what I set out to do. To my sister/built-in best friend Shannon McDonald Goldstein, thank you for being a defense attorney and helping me out of those two speeding tickets that I got a week apart on the same corner.

Thank you, Chelsea Handler. If it wasn't for your success and your example of hard work and perseverance, I would not be here today. I am so grateful for the past five years and for working for you on *Chelsea Lately*. And yes, working on *Chelsea Lately* is the most fun job ever mostly because I get to work with Tom Brunelle, Sue Murphy, Chuy Bravo, Brad Wollack, Sarah Colonna, Jen Kirkman, Chris Franjola, Jiffy Wild, Fortune Feimster, Steve Marmalstein, Josh Wolf, Dan

Maurio, Dan Brown, and April Richardson. You are more than just "The Others" to me, you are my friends for life, whether you have agreed to it or not.

I'd like to thank my incredible book agent and good friend Michael Broussard and his dog Dino, who is much healthier than Michael leads us to believe. To my awesome editor Matthew Benjamin, Kiele Raymond, Jessica Roth, Elisa Rivlin, and everyone else at Touchstone for making this book all that I dreamed it could become. Also to my managers at Roar, Jordan Tilzer and Bernie Cahill, everyone at William Morris Endeavor, Alex Spieller at IMPR, and Rich and Justin at Super Artists. Also to my special girl Sue Carswell aka my personal trainer, we'll always have Whitney. Dick Sanders who took my pregnant pics at www.DickSanders.com.

To my best friend Liz Killmond-Roman, who still has yet to miss a birthday party of mine. To Tara Klein for allowing me to call her every morning on my way to work to talk about our lives and the lives of the reality stars that intrigue us most. To my other dear girlfriends Kris Jenner, Maia Dreyer, Stacey Jenks, Anna Bercsi, Laney Ziv, and Lori Smith, I am so lucky to have attractive people surrounding me.

And to all my friends I've met through coming to my stand-up shows or on Facebook, Twitter, and Instagram, thank you. And thank you for reading this book and laughing at me.

ABOUT THE AUTHOR

Heather McDonald is a full-time writer, performer, and story producer on E! Channel's top rated show *Chelsea Lately,* and stars on the show's spin-off, *After Lately*. Heather is also a featured performer on *The Tonight Show with Jay Leno* and has been a guest star on the hit television series *Frasier, Malcolm in the Middle, Reno 911!,* and Nickelodeon's *Drake and Josh*. On the big screen, Heather cowrote *White Chicks* with the Wayans brothers and had a featured role in the film and in the Wayan's film *Dance Flick*. Heather's writing has also been featured in *Redbook* magazine, *Reader's Digest, The Hollywood Reporter* and she has contributed to *New York Magazine*'s *Vulture*. In addition, Heather continues to perform her stand-up at sold out shows across the country.

Heather has been married to her husband, Peter, for twelve years, with whom she has two sons and a stepdaughter. They reside in the San Fernando Valley next door to her parents just in case they run out of milk, Chardonnay, or need one of her dad's Vicodin.